Cracker Beach

From Hell to Heaven

Cracker Beach

From Hell to Heaven

David "Preacherman" Gaskill

CRACKER BEACH
From Hell to Heaven
© 2024 by David Gaskill

Printed in the United States of America.
ISBN-13: 979-82183927-1-0
Library of Congress Control Number: 2024905971

Fly Iggles Fly Publishing
Tampa, Florida

DEDICATION

To my 2 sons Adam and David "DJ" (on the right) for their strength, courage, and unconditional love, support, and friendship. They are my reason for living.

Pastor Tommy Kullonen

Pastor Bob Santilli

Pastor Chuck Smith

Dr. Tony Evans

Dr. Charles Stanley

AKNOWLEDGEMENTS

My Pastors Hall of Fame...

When I was released from jail, the first church I attended was Calvary Chapel in Brandon, Florida. The pastor there gave me a Chuck Smith study Bible. It remains my favorite source of truth and knowledge to this day.

Over the past 17 years I've attended many churches and listened to and watched many sermons, but the special men of God who I'd like to thank and acknowledge as having the biggest impact on my life are Pastor Smith, Doctor Tony Evans, Doctor Charles Stanley, Pastor Tommy Kyllonen, and Pastor Bob Santilli.

I met Pastor Bob in 1980 when I was a 19-year-old college dropout, but I didn't begin to get to know him until 2007 after Christ redeemed me. He was one of the first people I called from jail with the good news. I called him collect and he answered, ha ha, and I have been contacting him for wisdom, truth, and advice ever since. Whenever I have questions about Jesus, the scriptures, or life in general, he is my go-to. I consider him my mentor and my dear friend and I can't put into words how much he's meant to me and the Gaskill family as a whole.

Introduction

My name is David Scott Gaskill Sr. In August 2005, my wife of twenty-four years had finally decided she had had enough. She separated from me and moved from Burlington, New Jersey, 1000 miles away to Tampa, Florida. Within the next year and seven months, my wife was gone, my fifteen and twenty-year-old sons were gone, my dog Teddy was gone, my car was gone, my job of twenty-four years was gone, all of my money was gone, my entire retirement fund was gone, my house, along with everything in it was gone, my health was gone, and finally, my freedom was gone. This is my story.

What Went Wrong

What had happened to me? Where did my life go wrong? Where, or what was it, that had caused my moral values to disappear and my path to veer uncontrollably off course? There must be someone or something to blame, right?

Isn't there always a deeply embedded root cause that triggers deviant behavior? "The Son of Sam" went wacko when his neighbor's demon dog began conversing with him. Charles Manson's course became disarrayed when he believed he was Jesus, although I don't recall Jesus going off on an "acid trip" and murdering innocent families on a whim. It's assumed that Elvis was led to that fatal toilet by overwhelming fame and popularity, and although I was always fairly popular growing up, no one ever referred to me as "The King."

So, what was my excuse? What was my perfect alibi for exchanging the "American Dream" for a jail cell in what seemed like overnight? There must be one. There had to be, right? I couldn't have merely thrown away a life that most people could only dream of to venture to the gates of hell just by chance, right? It's almost as if I wanted to go there, or rather, I had to. It's almost as if I was compelled to visit the "pit." But why? How? What purpose could such needless pain possibly serve?

My Childhood

I grew up in a good Christian home in a small New Jersey town called Mount Holly with a silver spoon in my mouth. I never wanted or needed for anything. We went to the First United Methodist Church of Mount Holly every Sunday during my youth. My older brother and I even had been awarded the little gold perfect attendance pins to wear on the lapels of our little kiddie church suits. It was in that church that I had my first memorable encounter with God.

After Sunday school, I would often go upstairs to attend the adult service with my mom and dad. However, on this particular Sunday, I went with my grandmother Bird, my mom's mother. I was about six years old and went with Grammy Bird with the anticipation that she'd always reward me with a pack of Life Savers. We sat in our normal seats a few rows from the back, and I would lie down in the pew with my head on Grammy's lap and prepare for a nice morning nap.

I wasn't very fond of church. It wasn't just boring with the slow-motion lighting of the candle operas and the way-too-loud organ music played by an old lady with blue hair, but it was also very scary with the preacher walking up and down the aisles preaching hell and damnation.

However, this particular Sunday was different. As I lay there sucking on a cherry Life Saver, I began focusing intently on this beautiful stained-glass window with Jesus holding His hands out. The sun's rays were shining through the glass this particular morning, making it even more alluring, and I was almost in a trance-like state, mesmerized by Him. Jesus was staring right at me, and I couldn't take my eyes off Him. It felt like He just wanted to give me a hug, and I felt this warm peace come over me. I remember that warm feeling to this day.

I was always on the honor roll in school and was popular with all the kids, even the girls, although I was petrified of them until I was about eighteen. I was a three-sport phenom (baseball, basketball, football), a Rancocas Valley Regional H.S. Hall of Famer, and a baseball legend in my hometown. Shoot, just ask anybody, or just ask me, I was darn near the perfect kid.

My dad was the backbone of our family. He wasn't necessarily demanding, but he did expect his sons to be the best they could be at everything we did. He was very disciplined and incredibly consistent, possibly from his stint in the Army. We went to bed at the same time every night and got up at the same time each morning, with the exception of a couple of extra hours of leeway on the weekends to stay up and watch TV and to sleep in during the morning. He was a hard-working Christian father, often holding down two jobs, yet still managing to coach his sons' Little League teams. He was the most honest man I've ever met. I never remember him ever using a curse word except for an occasional "damn."

My mom, on the other hand, was the prototypical house wife and mother. She cooked three meals a day, day in and day out, did the laundry, kept the house spotless, had my brother and my uniforms always clean and ready for our next ballgame (a job in itself, considering we both played three sports all year round), and was always my emotional support. Her mother and father once lived on a farm, and I believe my mother and I inherited our love for animals from them. I was two or three years old when Mom took me to a lady's house down the street to see a litter of puppies. It was there that my dear mother let me pick out my first dog. We named her Lucky, but I was the one who was lucky to have a mother who recognized my over-the-top infatuation for animals almost from the time I could walk and let me have any kind of animal I ever wanted. I had rabbits, hamsters, turtles, and fish, and I fell head over heels in love with all of them, but Lucky was hands down my favorite. We had her for nearly twenty years, and I remember the day we had to have her put to sleep because of her failing health, and I remember my dad crying as he prayed and thanked God for blessing us with her as he buried her in our backyard. It was one of the few times I ever saw him cry. Lucky was a great companion and my best friend, and I never went to sleep at night until Lucky hopped into bed with me.

My brother, three years my senior, was the perfect older brother and my role model. If he got straight A's, I wanted to get straight A's. If he made the All-State team in baseball, I wanted to be All-State. I was always competing against the high standards that he set, and boy did he set them high. He never turned down a game of one-on-one with his little bro, be it wiffle ball, tennis ball, basketball, or ping pong. If there was a ball involved, we would go at it fiercely. He was extremely competitive, to say the least, even more so than me. He'd rather die than let his little brother beat him at anything, and those competitions pushed me to want to be better than him at everything I did, a goal I was never able to achieve.

Oh, the battles we had! Those were some of the very best times of my entire life, for sure. He set the bar extremely high for me, being a wonderful example as a student/athlete (University of Pennsylvania and R.V.R.H.S Hall of Fame baseball player), and person, who was, and still is, always there for me.

I never recall seeing anyone in my family ever drunk or high, and I believe it was because of the standards of integrity that my father had set. In fact, my brother, now sixty-six, who, according to the legend, has never as much smoked a joint in his entire life.

Then there's me, the black sheep of the family. I had never gotten in trouble as a youth or teen except for detention in second grade for talking in class, punishable by writing the sentence "I will not talk in class" 500 times, which, in fact, I never did again.

The superintendent of schools, a family friend, told my parents I was the happiest kid he'd ever seen. "Always smiling," he said. I remember others adding that I was the luckiest person they'd ever seen. Things always went my way.

I guess it was my secret Friend; it had to be.

You see, I began believing in God from the very beginning, as far back as I can remember. I had paid attention in Sunday school and knew all the stories—was fascinated by them, and although I knew about that guy named Jesus, I really didn't comprehend the whole "Father-Son-Holy Ghost" thing. I mean, who really does? Although Mom did have to wash my mouth out with soap on occasion, I was a darn good kid . . . just ask me. I even started reading my Bible in high school, prayed before meals and ball games, and always said the scripted "Now I lay me down to sleep, I pray the Lord my soul to keep . . ." prayer every night. I wanted people to see my faith, to know I was a "believer." Maybe it was out of pride or something. Maybe I wanted to be different or felt that I was special in some way. Only God Himself knows for sure, I guess.

So, when did things go astray? When did I start leaving an honest life and begin living a lie? When did I stop conversing with my best Friend and become swayed by the bad angel? When did I stop telling the truth and begin lying whenever it suited my purpose? I mean, it became so easy for me to lie, and I was exceptionally good at it. After all, I didn't feel like I was hurting anyone, except myself, of course.

I even cheated my employer, the one who gave me a shot as a nineteen-year-old college dropout with absolutely no job skills or training of any kind. I showed them my appreciation for blessing me with employment for twenty-four years by fudging hours on my weekly time cards pretty much every week. I didn't have to punch a clock, so I'd falsify the number of hours I worked, often putting down several hours of overtime in exchange for time that was spent surfing the Playboy sites on the internet.

I'd take my family to all the nicest restaurants for dinner and the best all-inclusive Caribbean resorts for our vacations, and then I'd come home and write them absolutely brilliant letters, completely degrading the places in an effort to get some freebies, and I always did. I made it sound like we had just visited purgatory itself, when, in fact, they were all absolutely amazing. We received gift certificates for dinners at expensive restaurants and Caribbean vacations to the five-star resorts of my choice.

I was so proud of my lying and cheating and would boast about my conquests to anyone who would listen. I mean, come on, I wasn't hurting anybody. All the organizations I was ripping off weren't hurting any, that's for sure, and I deserved it anyway. I was just trying to provide a better lifestyle for my family, right? Wrong! I was stealing man and didn't even care. What did the devil, the liar, the thief come for? He came "to steal, and to kill, and to destroy" (John 10:10). Hey, yes, I was a liar and a thief, but I never killed anyone, and the only thing I was destroying was my own soul, right?

When did I begin cheating everyone who meant anything to me? When did I start cheating myself, my own soul? I began lying to my wife, my kids, my parents, my brother, and everyone I would come in contact with, but worst of all, I was lying to myself. What had happened to my invisible Friend? The one Person I could always turn to when I was troubled with anything? The Person who ALWAYS comforted me and gave me peace and the strength to stay on the right track? The "good voice" within me that had been my conscience, the "voice" that I had ultimately always answered to as a child and as a young man?

Was it those excitingly wicked moments as a youth paperboy when I'd sneak behind the shed in our backyard to experiment with the cigarette butts that I had stumbled across during the day's deliveries? Although I choked viciously with each secret puff, I believe I received a degree of excitement in doing naughty. Who knows for sure? Maybe it was one of those filthy Camels that triggered the neurotransmitters in my head to go haywire. All I know is it had to be something that sent me reeling, right?

I suppose if you had to pick a time when my life went amiss, then it would have to be halfway through my freshman year at the University of Delaware. I never wanted to go there in the first place. I was a ball player, and from Little League on, I had set my sights on the Big Leagues. Scouts from several Major League teams had been attending my high school games, beginning when Dallas Green, the general manager of the Philadelphia Phillies, witnessed me throw a shutout at the varsity level my sophomore year. Hard-throwing left-handers were always a hot commodity, and the local newspapers listed me as one of the top prospects in New Jersey for the upcoming 1979 Major League Draft. The only question that remained now wasn't if I'd be drafted but how high would I be picked. However, the draft came and went without a call, and it devastated me.

The disappointment of not being selected stung my swagger and thoroughly rocked my world. I now knew how my brother had felt having also gone undrafted after setting several hitting records at Rancocas Valley High as well as the University of Pennsylvania. The stone cold reality of having to go off to college to have any chance of pursuing my dream had never been anywhere on my narrow radar. However, it was then my only option. I went on recruiting trips to the University of Miami, Duke, Wake Forrest, James Madison, Rutgers, and Rider University and was accepted at all of them, and although I was offered full scholarships to Rutgers and Rider, I finally decided to attend the University of Delaware, which had one of the top baseball programs in the northeast.

When I received an invite to try out from the Phillies in 1979 after my senior year in high school, I figured I would just bite my nose off to spite my face. I'd fix them for passing on me and not drafting the next Steve Carlton! My pride had been bruised, and since I was having so much fun shoveling human waste at the local Sewerage Authority, the summer job my dad had secured "to build my character"(boy, did it ever), I skipped the tryout. Even so, they still assured me that they would continue to follow my career as a "Blue Hen."

My college career started off according to the script. I made the varsity baseball team during "fall ball" (abbreviated season during Sept–Oct 1979) as a pitcher, and Head Coach Hannah talked about me being a starter in the spring. I was grudgingly going to class, but I was going and also passed them all.

A Trip That Rocked My World

After the season, I made a trip home to Mount Holly to visit my high school sweetheart. She was my first true love, I thought. She was a young lady I had gone to school with since elementary school. We had always been friends, and I knew she liked me, but it wasn't until my senior year in high school when she was nominated for homecoming queen that I noticed she had really blossomed as a young woman. She had an amazing smile and personality and sang in her church's choir, but it was when we began passing notes to each other in school that our relationship began to take off and we became a "thing." There was a complication, however. She was black, and I was white, and having grown up in a well-integrated town like Mount Holly, we didn't think anything about it. We didn't smoke or drink or use drugs and weren't in an intimate relationship. We were just two innocent kids enjoying each other's company. However, it was the seventies, and to the generation before us, interracial relationships were absolutely taboo.

People started talking. Nosy neighbors were calling my parents to inform them that they had seen us walking home from school together. Teachers and administrators at school began treating us differently. Once, while we chatted in the hallway between classes, the vice principal confronted us and sternly commanded us to "Break it up and get to class!"

Although our parents both loved us dearly, they also made it clear that our relationship was going to be a problem. "It's just not acceptable in this world," my dad informed me, and while her mother liked me, her father and older brother vehemently told her to end it.

Neither of us cared what others thought. We were crazy in love for the first time in our young lives and had been going steady for most of our senior year. The plan was I'd go off to college, become a pro baseball player, become rich and famous, and return home to sweep her off her feet, get married, and live happily ever after in a house with a white picket fence around it. Proverbs 16:9 says, "A man's heart plans his way, but the Lord directs his steps," and God was about to redirect my steps, along with the plans of my heart.

When I knocked on her front door to surprise her, I was the one who received the big surprise. She answered alright but had a young man draped around her, and sparing the details, it was obvious that they hadn't been playing Scrabble.

Crash, bang, pow! My whole world came crashing down. I had never experienced hurt like that before, my first truly broken heart. I was devastated. Wow! Man, did that smart! I felt like I was in shock or something. I could hardly breathe.

You must understand, my life had always been so sheltered. My parents were very strict with my brother and me, and for good reason. The world had begun changing way too quickly, and not for the best. The sixties and seventies were a bit of a crazy time, you know: the "Hippie" era, Vietnam, and so on, with its accompanied party mentality.

Yet, Mom and Dad did a great job of protecting us from it. Drugs, booze, and teenage sex had become commonplace with our generation, but my brother and I had been wisely instructed about the implications of partaking in any of them. Besides, we were both jocks with Major League aspirations and probably feared our dad's belt more than becoming a dope head or teenage "baby daddy" (parent).

After experiencing the London Bridge falling down right on top of my big blond-haired head, I turned around and headed back to the U. of D. like a dog with his tail between his legs to finish off my first semester. When I arrived, something had been stripped from me. I felt violated, so to speak. Please remember, I was now almost nineteen and had never smoked a joint or touched a beer in my life, even though the drinking age was eighteen in New Jersey in 1979. I was a "party virgin," I guess you would say, and although my Bible sat comfortably on my dorm room dresser, the distractions of college life and the freedom of being on my own for the first time in my life had severely weakened my "shield," my "armor." I didn't suppose my dad's belt could see me or find me all the way down in Newark, Delaware, and my hurt was blocking the comforting voice, wisdom, and direction of my once best Friend. I was alone, felt alone, and wanted the hurt of being cheated on and losing my first real girlfriend to go away and go away quickly.

So, I did it. I sought out my best friend in the dorm, Henry. Henry was a lot of fun, the dorm clown, a very goofy dude who resembled Ringo Star and had the most amazing Tectonics stereo and sound system, although it wasn't music I was looking for. I wanted to get "high," you know, "Panama Red," "Jamaican Gold," "weed," and everyone knew Henry loved his dope. So I went straight to his room, found him there, high as usual, and semi-proudly said, "Henry, I wanna get high."

Oh, those infamous words that would rock my entire being. If only I had any idea of the impact they would have on the course of my destiny. He smiled goofily and questioned, "You, David, you?" You see, I was pretty much the only "straight" guy on the entire dorm floor, maybe the entire dorm, and I was proud of it. I couldn't "defile the temple," right? Granted, it wasn't easy since walking the halls of Rodney D (our dorm) was like walking into the Scooby-Doo fog, if you know what I mean. There was always a thick cloud of marijuana smoke that you could practically cut with a knife. You could nearly get high just sitting in the dorm commons watching TV, which I avoided at all costs, but that day was gonna be the day I'd lose my "party virginity," and my bud Henry was only more than obliged to make it happen. He pulled out his big blue mega bong and a big bag of "grass" and started loading it up.

Henry was a well-off kid whose parents owned a big manufacturing company, and like everything else he had, his bong was top of the line.

Here we go! He loaded up a monster hit for me and instructed me on the proper technique of not only how to hold the instrument of mass destruction but also how to take a hit and then hold the smoke deep in my lungs before exhaling. I was a quick learner, no doubt. Although I thought I was gonna choke to death after my first hit, before I knew what had hit me, or what I had hit, should I say, I was rolling around on Henry's bunk laughing hysterically as "My Sharona" blared on his stereo.

Isn't it weird how we remember those special life-changing moments? To say I was high would be a major understatement. I COULD NOT STOP laughing! As I lay there almost paralyzed, the entire dorm was standing outside Henry's dorm room laughing with me, or at me, I don't know and didn't care, and Henry was jumping around with his arms raised and screaming over me like Ali after defeating Sonny Listen. The "Holly Hummer" (my self-proclaimed baseball nickname) was high!

I could sympathize with Goliath when he got hit in the head with that rock. Although I was also hit in the head in a much more pleasurable way and still alive to talk about it, I knew something inside me had truly died. There was no "good voice" anymore, or at least I couldn't hear or feel it anyway.

There was now a new sheriff in town, who I'm sure was always there within my head, and although I had been able to ignore his voice up to this point, it was only because of my parents' tutelage and the guidance, power, and influence of my former best Friend.

I had a new friend now, the kinda friend my parents had worked so hard to shelter my brother and me from. My new "bestie" was called addiction.

Instantly an Addict

According to the National Institute on Alcohol Abuse and Alcoholism (NIAAA) 10 percent of Americans have had a drug use disorder at some time in their lives, and unfortunately, I happened to be one of those one out of ten people who was cursed with an addictive personality and instantly became an addict.

Immediately after that initial indiscretion, I thought that it was the greatest thing I had ever experienced in my life! It blew Disney's Space Mountain right off the chart! Shoot, I could now almost talk to a pretty girl without stuttering. If I had only known while I was in high school, maybe I would have been Prom King or at least have gone to the prom. Absolutely nothing mattered to me anymore at this point except for getting high somehow, some way, all day, every day.

Looking back, the guys on my dorm floor must have hated seeing me coming. I would pace the floor, knocking on every door I could find, looking for a "pot party," and never have a problem finding one. I think I actually thought I'd smoke weed for free for the rest of my life. However, the boys caught on to my scheme and put a squash to that pipe dream real quick and began charging me. No problem, I just used the money I made from the college work-study program I was in. That's what it was for, right?

Although I certainly enjoyed weed, and rolling up a couple "fatties" (joints) had become as commonplace to me as brushing my teeth, the pleasure sensors of my mind had been thoroughly teased, and I was now thirsting, literally and figuratively, for another new experience, a new high, another level, a higher high, so to speak.

The Party Animal

Fraternity parties were prevalent at school, and near the end of my first semester, I began to frequent them with my newfound buddies, all of whom drank beer, of course.

The smell and taste of beer had always been a turnoff to me, so I would meander around at the parties with a cup of "suds" in my hand, gagging it down a sip at a time.

Someone had told me once that beer was an acquired taste, kinda like sushi was, and boy, were they right. Just like dope, I acquired a taste for beer pretty much overnight. Boy, oh boy, did I start loving me some beer! I quickly advanced from sipping to chugging it down like John Belushi in *Animal House*, and although I noticed I had a high tolerance for it compared to my friends, I always had to be the drunkest one at the end of the night. I don't know why. Pride maybe? Maybe the competitive nature my brother and I had inherited from our dad (a former professional baseball player)—who knows? All I know is I wanted to out-smoke and out-drink everybody else, and I always did. Looking back on my mythic binges, I have to wonder if my nearly unlimited tolerance was a blessing from God to protect me from killing myself or a curse from Satan to drive me to kill myself? I suppose only they know for sure.

The Wrong Circle of Friends

When it was time to head back home to Mount Holly for winter break (early December 1979), the metamorphosis of the Holly Hummer must have caught everyone by surprise. Any respect that I had earned in high school for being a righteous role model for my peers quickly dissipated. All my former closest friends, a circle of about a dozen, who were all straight and narrow student-athletes, quickly became a distant memory. I specifically sought out, like a heat-seeking missile, the "problem children," the very ones I had avoided in my "other" life in my effort to remain in "highdom" during the winter break.

Suddenly, I was one of the boys now, and having gone from being voted the shyest person in Rancocas Valley High School class of 1979, I was now on a mission to conquer every girl who had ever smiled at me, and I pretty much did.

My life had always been one of all or nothing (a characteristic of addicts), and now I had gone from complete abstinence in every way to completely obnoxious in every way. I had now become one of those very people I had always been determined to never become.

I distinctly remember my dad asking me during one of our weekly family Friday night pizza dinners, "Why can't you drink just one beer?" I also distinctly remember not having a rebuttal for him but also thinking to myself, "What would possibly be the purpose of drinking only one beer? What would be the fun in that?"

My beautiful father. Dear ole Dad could have a couple of slices of Sal's pie and one beer, and he was content. For him to sincerely ask me that question could only mean one thing. He obviously wasn't a drunk like me, and neither was my mother. Thank You, God!

I doubt that they ever even noticed that the VO in the Seagram's bottle that they stored under their stereo cabinet for their occasional Bridge party had been secretly replaced with H2O by the family booze hound.

The Dream Was Over

When I returned to the U. of D. for the spring semester of my freshman year, my dream of becoming my high school's first Major League Baseball player was a mere afterthought.

The partying didn't seem to be much of a problem at first. I mean, it was college; that's what you did, right? And although it didn't appear to be affecting the other players, it was certainly affecting me.

My course to the Big Leagues was now diverted by my choice to live the "high life." My psyche was beginning to erode, and my conscience was eating away at me. I had lost my focus, my edge.

From the time I was a Little Leaguer, my opponents couldn't touch me, and that continued all the way through my initial college fall season. Yet, in the spring of 1980, I was no longer a "big fish in a little pond." I was more like a fish out of water.

By dropping my guard and allowing the devil to sneak in the back door, his chief weapon discouragement was now running rampant within my mind. I began doubting my ability to perform as an athlete, as a student, and even as a person.

I was deeper into the party scene now, and the boys, many of whom were my teammates on the fall baseball team, and I could always find one somewhere. We'd party all night, then if we were too hungover in the morning, we'd simply skip class and sleep in, at least I would, since baseball practices were in the afternoon during the week.

There were two major flaws to this plan, however. One, I was beginning to skip class way more than I was going, and two, Coach Hannah had been coaching college ball for a long time and knew that to keep his team sharp and on their toes, he would schedule the weekend practices for 7:00 a.m., regardless if it were fall, winter, or spring, and they ALWAYS began with running drills. Ouch! I can still remember dragging myself to the Blue Hen Dome (indoor facility) with my eyes half falling out of my head and the smell of beer and vomit still fresh on my breath from the previous night's escapades.

Until you become a well-seasoned drunk, and I was well on my way at this point, you have to experience a ton of "hugging the porcelain god" (throwing up in the toilet), and I was a regular puker. There's also no crueler punishment for an undisciplined college baller than running laps at the break of dawn with "cotton mouth" (dry mouth from marijuana).

It's been over forty years since the U. of D. glory days, but I still sometimes wonder if the coach had any suspicions about his "wild bunch." Even if he did, I'm not so sure how much it bothered him, considering we went 33-13 that spring, won the East Coast Conference, and came within one win of the College World Series.

Just as the Saturday morning "nightmares" (practices) began to wear on me, I was introduced to a new savior, amphetamines, or as they were commonly referred to, "speed" or "black beauties" (methamphetamine). What a blessing, I thought. I had been kind of wondering how the seniors on the team, many of whom partied all night with us freshman, could show up on Saturday morning for practice looking fresh, like they had spent the night at the convent. Yup, black beauties. Apparently, they were popping them like jelly beans, so we figured, or I figured, I should say, "What's good for the goose is good for the gander."

Beauties were cheap and broke the ground for my soon-to-be and future pill-popping propensity. You could get ten for a buck, so there was now no reason to catch any sleep whatsoever on party nights. Beauties did much more than wake you up and give you an energy drink type of boost, however. The blood-thinning effect from the amphetamine didn't just make abusers run like deer, but it also greatly enhanced the throwing ability of us pitchers, although I'm not sure I can supply scientific evidence to that effect.

I fell so in love with amphetamines that I rarely practiced or played without their assistance. That was one of the biggest mistakes that I've made in a lifetime filled with poor judgment.

I had been throwing for weeks under the influence of beauties, and because of their numbing effect, I was unable to discern how my arm was really feeling.

I remember like yesterday when I told Coach Hannah that it was "feeling funny"; almost dead would be a better description. He promptly sent me to the school athletic doctor to get checked out. To make a long story short, I was diagnosed with shoulder tendinitis, and having been unable to decipher the pain in my arm, I had continued throwing and consequently damaged my rotator cuff to the point that I had to begin a weekly regime of therapy and cortisone shots.

My role on the team seemed to evaporate almost immediately and, along with it, any chance I had of being in the starting pitching rotation.

Coach, against my wishes and considering my future as a pitcher, was very careful in his pampering of me. I only pitched sparingly that initial season, mostly in relief. He did bless me one sunny Saturday morning with a start against Georgetown University, in which I revisited my glory days by promptly shutting them out for five innings and receiving my first college victory. Who knew that would be my first and last start as a pitcher for the University of Delaware?

No Baseball for the Summer

The summer of 1980 was very unique for me. Coach Hannah advised me to take the summer off from pitching, hoping that rest would be the best therapy for my dead arm. That would be the first summer since I was seven years old that I didn't play baseball. I didn't really miss it, to be honest.

My life had a new purpose, and it wasn't working on my curve ball grip, that's for sure. I just wanted to party and chase after women, and that's pretty much all Spanky and the gang did (me and my band of nitwits).

A friend of my mother secured me a job at 38 Liquors, a very popular local liquor store on Route 38 in Mount Holly. It turned out to be the perfect summer job for an alcoholic in the making. I literally was a "taste tester" that summer. I could experiment with just about any kind of liquor known to man without spending a dime. It was just too easy. I would sneak a couple of "airplane shot" bottles into my pocket, then simply head to the bathroom in the back of the store for a quick "pop" or sneak them into a can of soda to sip while I worked. Gin, rum, vodka, tequila, Jack Daniels, Johnny Walker, Wild Turkey, you name it, and I had access to them all, tasted them all, and decided that Bacardi rum and coke would be my cocktail of choice for life.

Mr. Popular

During one hot summer day at the store, I became the thing that legends are made of, or should I say that residents of San Quentin are made of? One of my many functions as a clerk for the store was handling the liquor truck deliveries. The trucks would pull up and park by the back door (storage room area), which was where we stored any product that didn't go straight into the freezer, refrigerator, or onto the shelves in the main store. Since the location of 38 Liquors (in the center of a very popular area of town called Lumberton Plaza) made it extremely popular and busy, deliveries arrived throughout the day. Hence, keeping an accurate record of the inventory was of the utmost importance to keep the store stocked and functioning efficiently. It was my job to unload the trucks, make a count of each item, check it in against the truckers' "packing list," and then sign for the shipment upon completion. This was a fairly important task for a nineteen-year-old college student, but I relished the responsibility and appreciated the faith shown me by store management, a trust they would later regret.

After becoming thoroughly versed in the store procedures and always one to daydream, I devised a scheme to pull off the biggest heist since *The Brink's Job*. It started when I was taking out the trash one day. No one was around, so as I carried out the empty boxes, I also carried out a full case of Heineken and deposited it in the trash dumpster. I knew the trash truck didn't come until the morning, so when my shift was over, I drove my car around behind the building and picked up my free case of Heiny's! Needless to say, the nitwits and I drank real good that night.

It was way too easy. So, the guys figured if it was that easy to "cop" a case of beer, why not go for the gusto? Well, to us junior alcoholics, the gusto was champagne. The summer before, I was the one preaching not to submit to peer pressure, now here I was not wanting to be a party popper or break any of our unwritten gang initiation codes, so I went for it. To make a long story short, every girl I dated that summer was treated to a bottle of Andre sparkling champagne. Mr. Quietest of the 1979 R.V. senior class sure was becoming Mr. Popular mighty quick.

There's Gotta Be More

Taking the summer off from baseball may have helped heal my arm a bit, but spending my free time running the streets with Rick, Ralph, and Wimpy made me sick in a way I'll never be able to explain. Although I can never blame anyone for the corruption that had invaded my soul, not even the devil himself, I learned what N.A. (Narcotics Anonymous) and A.A. (Alcoholics Anonymous) meant by teaching the importance of avoiding "people, places, and things." Scripture also wisely advises us, "Evil company corrupts good habits" (1 Cor. 15:33). I had even begun believing that the worst of friends were also the most loyal friends, and drugs had unlocked some secret door in my mind that contained all the secrets of knowledge. Go figure those words of wisdom.

Better Living Through Chemicals

When I returned to school that fall (1980), my downward spiral into addiction was picking up speed at an alarming rate.

One of my loving teammates introduced me to Quaaludes (methaqualone). A Quaalude was a cute white pill marked "Lemon 714," about twice the size of an aspirin, and was the polar opposite of the black beauty.

Quaaludes were "downers", which, taken along with alcohol, had the effect of a six-pack of beer on a person within an hour. Boy, oh boy, I should have majored in chemistry. I was truly becoming a chemical engineer overnight without the need to attend the corresponding boring classes.

I now had pretty much all of the bases covered, no pun intended, at least so I thought. I had something to bring me down at night from the amphetamine high and then something to lift me up in the morning from the beer/Quaalude hangover.

My contentment was short-lived, however. I began to completely boycott my college courses to expand my knowledge of the only course that had any relevance in my life, "Better Living Through Chemicals." If only they had awarded credits for that course, then I would have had my master's in a semester.

Still Searching

I needed something to continue tickling my brain's pleasure sensors to keep my serotonin (the brain's happy-feeling chemical) and endorphins (the brain's pain-killing chemical) pumping at a record rate, so I began experimenting with everything and anything.

Since graduation from uppers, downers, weed, and booze was now complete, I enrolled in an all-out assault on hallucinogens. First, it was "magic mushrooms," then LSD ("acid"), and then for the ultimate killer of brain cells, nitric oxide, or laughing gas.

There may have been others, but I just can't remember. In fact, the only thing I can remember about the fall ball season that had to do with baseball was getting so wasted on ludes and booze-watching George Thorogood perform at "The Stone Balloon" (an on-campus saloon) that I flipped butt over backward off my bar stool and was ushered out. It wasn't until the next day that I realized I had left my cherished University of Delaware Varsity Championship jacket on that same bar stool.

To think that precious moment was bad, things would only get worse. I was taking hallucinogens as often as I could get my hands on them and was completely losing touch with reality.

One day, while my friend Charles and I were high on mushrooms and watching fluorescent butterflies floating about his dorm room, we devised the perfect plan. We would drop out of school right then and there, move to Orlando, Florida, and get a job at Disney World, you know, a ticket taker or something. Then just chill, high as a kite, and watch the rides go round and round. Man, that would be the ultimate!

Charles backed out, though. It seemed he was actually in school to get a degree or something.

Something Was Missing

Partying, although exciting at first, was beginning to feel like everything else I had experienced in my life up to that point. Be it sports, school, or girlfriends, I was always left feeling like, "Is this it? Is this all there is? There has got to be more to this life than this."

As far back as I could possibly remember, I always had a feeling within me of unfulfillment, followed by disappointment.

There was an emptiness, a void, that I was afraid could never be filled. Sports were fun and consumed most of my youth, and although there were many great moments, they never filled it. Girls couldn't fill it, no matter how pretty they were, darn it. In some sadistic way, I guess I thought there must be a high out there somewhere that would be the "it" for me, the missing link to fulfillment, and I was insanely driven to find it.

I kept this dark secret to myself for the sole reason that, as I stated previously, I felt different in some way. Maybe weird would be more like it. I thought people would think I was a little cuckoo or something, especially if they knew that I only shared my concerns, my most intimate secrets, with my invisible, secret Friend. I was determined to find out what "it" was. I had to. I felt that my existence in this world depended upon it, but the problem was that the void within me, the emptiness, was only getting bigger the more I searched to fill it. It's kinda like it must feel when you get stuck in quicksand, I suppose. The harder you struggle, the deeper you sink. But I kept reaching and was determined to find that "branch" that was gonna pull me out.

Depression

began feeling so terribly alone, even more so than before, and was beginning to experience my first taste of depression.

The depression escalated my drinking, and my drinking, being a depressant, escalated my depression, if that makes sense. I had launched my self-destructive personality to scary heights. I was trying to run away from myself, yet it was like running from my own shadow. I was so disappointed with myself and what I had become and was becoming.

This wasn't me! This wasn't the Holly Hummer! I felt like an airplane that had been hit and was spiraling out of control down toward earth. I was going to have to come down (sober up), sooner or later, and face the real world with its responsibilities, but I was planning on procrastinating that point as long as possible, if not forever. I was inevitably going to crash. It was just a matter of when, where, how, and could I possibly survive it.

The Party of All Parties

I had an idea, even better than the Disney ticket-taker brainstorm. I would host the party of all parties! Everyone on campus would be invited. It would be a great way for me to meet people, make new friends, increase my popularity, and show off my partying prowess.

I began spreading the word. I told all my friends and told them to tell their friends. There would be plenty of food, even shrimp, a keg of beer, liquor, weed, assorted drugs of every kind, and best of all, unlike other campus parties, no cover charge. This would be "it." I just knew it.

Money was no object for this budding Hugh Hefner. My dad had been nice enough to open a bank account for me at school and deposited the money from my student loan in it. A couple thousand smackers were at my beckoning call. Oh, the beauty of bank cards! Free money, I thought. Who knew you had to pay it back?

Although, that fact of reality didn't really matter to me. I was planning on disappearing soon anyway. I had no idea where; Disney still sounded good, but I had better go somewhere because when my dad found out I had blown all of my loan money and failed all my classes, there would be no welcome home party, that's for sure.

When it was time for the big day, I began preparing for the party early in the afternoon. By that, I mean that I started partying for the party early in the afternoon. I made up a couple of pitchers full of grain alcohol punch and began chugging it as if it were Kool-Aid. I also had a handful of shrooms for lunch, a couple of ludes, a couple of beauties, and by 2 or 3 o'clock, had the stereo pumping and was well "baked" (high).

An old high school sweetheart of mine came all the way from Rutgers University for the big blowout. Looking back, we both began gulping the Kool-Aid a bit early, I suppose.

Sundown had come and gone, and it was still only the two of us slipping into the abyss. I was getting more and more anxious, waiting and wondering where everyone was at.

As the evening came to a standstill, I was feeling totally worthless and so totally alone. The feeling of emptiness was overwhelming. I wanted so much to be accepted into the "party fraternity" of my peers. I learned what it must have felt like for a little kid who had had a birthday party and had his heart set on the presents, but no one showed up to give him any.

As midnight approached, it was apparent that there would be no Times Square ball-dropping celebration; in fact, it would be the exact antithesis thereof.

With only complete and final destruction in mind, I inhaled the last few grams of mushrooms, followed by a big glass of punch. My dorm room started spinning, and although I had been hallucinating for hours from the mushrooms, the hallucinations became more horrific and led me to strong suicidal urges. I was engulfed with fear, anger, and depression, all at the same time, and did the first logical thing of the day. I picked up the phone and called my parents.

I remember the first words out of my mom's mouth clearly. "What's wrong?"

I sobbed, "Please come and get me. I think I'm gonna kill myself."

She quickly snapped back, "We're on our way!"

They arrived at my dorm room an hour later to get their first glimpse of hell. They rescued me that night, surely saved my life and possibly even my soul.

As I look back, I feel so sorry for any child who would have to grow into adulthood without having two loving parents to give them unconditional love. I'm so thankful and blessed to have always received that from my mother and father.

Time to Dry Out

When I got back to Mount Holly to detox at my parents' house, my brother came home from the University of Penn to be with me. We had always been very close as kids but had gotten separated a bit when he went off to college. He quickly reinforced the fact that he would always be there whenever I needed him, and he has always kept faithful to that promise.

I'm not sure if he was on winter break or not, but he stayed there at my parents' house with me for at least a couple of weeks. During that time, I confessed to him that I had a serious problem with addiction. I told him how it had started and that I didn't believe I could ever drink or use any kind of drugs again without it going very badly for me. I remember he also confessed that he had gotten drunk on occasion at college with his roommates, and although many of them smoked pot as well, he never had. I was so amazed at his honesty. He was always my role model, and for him to express some of his exploits to me caught me completely off guard.

I had been feeling so terribly alone, and for my brother to admit that he wasn't the absolute perfect individual that I had always envisioned was very uplifting to me. I realize now how unselfish it was of him to willingly put himself down to help lift me up, and it truly gave me a much-needed emotional lift.

A Talk with Coach

After drying out for a couple of weeks, my father drove me back to the U. of D. to discuss my situation with Coach Hannah and to apologize. Coach was an amazing man in every way, almost larger than life to some of us players, and it was easy to understand why he was so successful.

I remember sitting in his office, staring at all the championship plaques and team pictures on the wall, and being in utter awe. I did not know what to say, so I just drooped my head and, holding back tears, said, "I'm sorry, Coach." He didn't want my apology; all he was concerned about was my well-being and getting better. He said he was proud of me for admitting I had a problem, for seeking help, and that if I decided to return to school in the spring, he would welcome me back to the team with open arms. I was so relieved by his kindness, and I'm sure my father was as well.

Alcoholics Anonymous

At my parents' urging, I attended an AA meeting at the Catholic church on Washington Street in Mount Holly with my dad. I'm not sure I did it with the intention of recovering as much as to give them some assurance.

After several lost souls confessed their horror stories related to their "illness," it was my turn to raise my hand and humbly state, "I'm David, and I'm an alcoholic." It was easy for me to say and actually felt good, but the look I witnessed on my dad's slightly bowed head was one of pure devastation.

Yes, I was an alcoholic and had accepted it, but I didn't want my dad to have to accept the same reality. As we walked through the parking lot after the meeting, I remember thinking to myself, "What a bunch of losers!" I assured him, "I'm not like those guys, Dad. I don't think these meetings are for me."
I don't recall if he even responded, but the truth was that I was exactly like every one of those men that night.

I Wasn't Ready for School

After a month of sobriety, I informed my dad that I didn't want to return to Delaware in the spring. I said that the fall semester was a possibility, but not the spring. I simply wasn't ready to handle all the temptations there. Although I know he was so disappointed and wanted so badly for me to fulfill his own dream of being a Major League baseball player, he never expressed it. He showed me other options to explore, such as trade schools and so on, and I actually did attend one a few months later called Lincoln Technical Institute, which was located in nearby Pennsauken, New Jersey, to study electronics, but it only lasted about a month or so.

Fate

In the meantime, however, my father was running out of options and patience for me and told me I needed to find employment if I wasn't returning to school. I didn't know why at the time, but I headed straight to a nearby McDonald's to fill out a job application. A girl I recognized, who was a cheerleader for my high school basketball team, happened to be working there. She also happened to be dating the manager of the store and put in a good word for me.

I was hired a couple of days later. I was so proud to have found employment so quickly, although I again don't believe a "burger flipper" was what my dad had envisioned for his Major League hopeful; destiny is often too wonderful to understand.

I have always felt that everything happens for a reason, but the way the "worm turned" for me during a most trying period in my young life was so extraordinary that it could have become a made-for-TV fairy tale.

During the next couple of weeks as a "grill master," I kept noticing a very pretty young waitress on the other side of the grill counter looking kind of funny at me. She just happened to be the younger sister of the girl who got me the job there. I'm also pretty sure she probably noticed that I was looking kind of funny at her as well.

I had first noticed her when I was in my early teens while she practiced cheerleading near a baseball field that I was playing at. Having always been intimidated by pretty girls, especially one as captivating as her, I never approached her, even though the first time I laid eyes on her, I felt something. I wasn't sure what it was at the time, but she was different. Maybe it was the way she uniquely rested her sunglasses up on top of her head, or maybe it was simply the fact that she had the most stunning big brown eyes I had ever seen. All I know is that she seemed different than other girls.

It was the beginning of December 1980, while I was working at that McDonald's, that I received a phone call that would wonderfully change the course of my destiny. I no longer had to worry about approaching the pretty, brown-eyed cheerleader/McDonald's waitress any longer; it was her on the phone.

She asked me if I'd like to go see a movie with her and her girlfriend Andy, who just happened to also be the girlfriend of my friend Wimpy. I immediately said yes.

It was a fun double date that night at the movies. I didn't get to talk with her much there, but I was the driver, so I strategically drove Andy and Wimpy home first to end the evening with quiet time with my date. Needless to say, my father didn't raise a fool.

As we sat in the parking lot on the side of her parents' house (which also doubled as her father's barbershop) that beautiful starlit night, we talked for what seemed like forever. Neither of us wanted the date to end, but her parents had given her a curfew, and we were getting dangerously close to it.

So we said our goodbyes, and I leaned across the seat and gave her our first goodnight kiss.

We instantly became a couple, and little did I know that I would not only never forget the touch of that first kiss, but from that moment on, I would rarely ever go another moment the rest of my life without her on my mind. It was certainly meant to be, and we knew it.

Career Change

I only had to wear my way undersized skintight baby blue McDonald's uniform with the appropriated blue and white paper sailors hat for a couple of months before my girlfriend's dad found me a job working for a customer of his installing wood fencing. It was backbreaking work, but I grew to enjoy its physical nature as well as being outside amongst nature.

My big break came in October 1981. My brother had been working about a year or so for a company called Consarc Corporation, located ten minutes away in Rancocas, New Jersey, which engineered and manufactured Vacuum Induction Melting furnaces for the specialty metals industry. He informed me that they were looking for shop workers (shipping/receiving), so I promptly went and applied. A good friend of his was the shipping foreman and hired me right on the spot. My big brother always did have a way of watching out for me like a guardian angel.

I had zero experience in manufacturing; however, the shipping foreman and the shop foreman liked the fact that I had a physique that would perfectly fit the requirements for the position. It was definitely a step in the right direction.

The job was minimum wage but included benefits that the other job didn't (dental and health insurance, paid holidays, vacation, time and a half for overtime, profit-sharing bonuses, and retirement plan).

I started out as a crate builder. The company was very busy, and we were shipping pretty much all over the country as well as the world. My job was to construct wooden crates for the various assemblies, and for the first month or so, that was all I did, day in and day out.

The shipping foreman and I hit it off very well, and his boss, Mr. Jones (purchasing manager), also took a special liking to me. I wasn't afraid of hard work and was hungry to make my mark. They quickly gave me my first promotion as I took over the shipping and receiving clerk duties and was responsible for all incoming and outgoing freight.

After working in the shop for only three months, Mr. Jones offered me a job working for him in the purchasing department as an MRO (Material Requisition Ordering) buyer. It was another promotion, another increase in pay, and my first white collar job. I had my own cubicle in the same department as my brother, which allowed us to spend a lot of quality time discussing the daily morning sports pages as well as other completely nonwork-related topics. We were closer than we had been in years, and I believe Mom and Dad were not only very proud of my progress but also must have felt some relief from my not-so-distant turmoil-filled past.

Ralph the Miracle Dog

A short while after beginning my employment at Consarc, while eating in the lunchroom, I noticed a stray dog that kept wondering up outside the lunchroom door, looking for scraps.
He appeared to be some sort of a German shepherd mix. He was terribly undernourished and had possibly been abused. We (the employees) all tried approaching him in an effort to feed him, but he wouldn't come within a stone's throw of anyone. We began opening the door and leaving bologna sandwiches and various treats outside, then we'd shut the door and watch as he happily would sneak up and grab his fill, then run back out into the surrounding woods to feast.

As we slowly began winning his trust, we started leaving the door open until "Ralph" finally began joining us for lunch. He took a real liking to all the men and women at Consarc, and we all enjoyed his gentle demeanor. It appeared he appreciated having some sort of a family after living solo in the woods for who knows how long.

As we worked in the shipping department building crates, we would leave the entrance door open to give ole Ralph a place to come in out of the heat. We always had a bowl of fresh water set up for him, and if we could have trusted him with a nail gun, we probably would have put him to work. Ralph was one of the boys now.

It wasn't unusual for him to wander the entire plant to greet the guys in each department. It was nice having a company mascot and watchdog for a while, but when Ralph began getting too comfortable with his new home, problems began arising.

Although we had made a pen for him to sleep inside at night, he began leaving his business pretty much wherever he felt the need. It was pretty evident that Ralph hadn't been housebroken.

Since he took a special liking to me and was considered by most to be my adopted son, I was the one given the heart-wrenching task of finding Ralph a new forwarding address, or he would have to be taken to the city pound. I promptly put an ad in the local newspaper and received many inquiries about the "German shepherd needing a good home." When I finally found a suitable candidate and arrangements were made for him to be picked up, Ralph was nowhere to be found. Did he sense that he was getting the boot, or did God have a greater purpose for him?

Ralph loved roaming the cornfield and woods that surrounded the Consarc facility, so I began a brief half-hearted search. As I drove down to the end of the long driveway that served as the entrance and exit to the plant, I found him. He was lying flat in the grass a few feet off of the main highway. I quickly sensed something was terribly wrong . . . he wasn't moving. He had been hit by a car or truck and was in a state of shock. His eyes were fixed, and his tongue hung uselessly out of the side of his mouth as he panted desperately.

I called for a fellow employee to help me lift him into the company station wagon. The old man who helped me was crying terribly, and so was I.

I drove as fast as I could to a local emergency veterinary clinic and begged them to help my friend. They rushed him inside for X-rays, and after much evaluation, it was determined he had a shattered pelvis, a broken rear femur, and was bleeding internally. The doctor suggested he be put to sleep. I pleaded with the doctor, "Please save my dog!" He said he couldn't guarantee that Ralph would survive the surgery, and even if he did, he didn't know what condition he would be in.

After receiving permission from Mr. Jones to do "whatever needs to be done for Ralph," I signed the consent form, and they operated. I'm not sure if I have ever begged God so hard for a favor as I did that day, but He heard me and answered my cries, and there sure was a lot of crying.

After having a plate screwed into his hip to hold his pelvis together and a metal rod inserted to stabilize his leg, Ralph survived. It was obviously too soon to tell, but because of the extent of the damage to his rear right hind leg, it was quite possible that he wouldn't regain use of it. I was also informed that he may never bark again due to the shock of suffering such a traumatic incident.

His recovery seemed to take forever as he broke his stitches on several occasions and continually had to fight off infection from the surgeries. During one of the follow-up visits, the doctor informed me that they would have to remove the limp leg or risk it getting infected with gangrene, which could spread and eventually take his life. I told the doctor I had seen signs of movement in the leg, but he insisted that is was merely nerve twitches. Nevertheless, he gave me some more time to decide.

Then it happened. On a perfect sunny Saturday afternoon, I took Ralph for a trip to the two-acre lawn in front of Consarc, where he loved to run (I had adopted him and taken him home after his recovery). As I lay there on the grass playing fetch with him, we spotted a hot air balloon hovering off in the distance. When Ralph noticed it, he began running with all four legs after it, jumping and barking! I began yelling out to him, "Ralph, you're barking! You're barking, boy!" Although his formally limp hind leg wasn't as good as new, it was functioning again and remained a part of Ralph for the nearly twenty years that he was a beloved member of our family.

As I've said, I always knew there was a God and certainly felt Him tugging at my heart to commit my life to Him, but I didn't know God. Let me repeat. I knew there was a God, but I didn't know God and certainly didn't know His Son Jesus. Maybe the sole purpose of meeting Ralph and witnessing the miracle healing of his horrific injuries was only to remind me once again that my best Friend was always with me, right there on that lawn, and that something much greater than each of us was still in control of all things.

Winning My Girlfriend's Parents' Approval

My girlfriend's parents also seemed impressed with my new white collar appearance. At first meeting, I believe they were very apprehensive concerning my intentions with their youngest daughter. Mount Holly was a very small town and had laid claim to being the "Gossip Capital of the World." It was obvious by the interrogations I was subjected to at their family's kitchen table that they had caught wind of some Holly Hummer tales that had been swirling about town for quite a while, namely that I had been in an interracial relationship.

They were churchgoers and professed to be Christians, so I expected them to be perfect. You know, forgive and forget, love, and all that stuff, my mistake for sure. Although, I am pretty sure that they, like many Christians I had come across, unknowingly put family before God's jealousy to be numero uno. At times, they appeared more interested in crucifying me than entering martyrdom themselves. However, it would be in violation of the "in-law-to-be and son-in-law-to-be privilege" to disclose the content of those discussions. They certainly had every right to learn as much about me as they could.

Their daughter was very special; they knew it and desired nothing but the best for their youngest daughter. Although I've never had a daughter and did not understand it then, I certainly appreciate their paranoia now. However, I was no longer the minimum-wage-earning college dropout drug addict they had probably dreaded from the first moment they had laid eyes on me. Well, at least I wasn't earning minimum wage anymore anyway.

If they weren't impressed with my new elevated social status as a businessman, they surely must have been ecstatic that I was accompanying them and their daughter to their Pentecostal church in Burlington, New Jersey, three times a week (Sunday morning and evening and Wednesday nights).

Boy, did I hate church! Putting a dollar in the offering plate each service hurt more than anything I had ever experienced in my life to that point, and hearing people yelling out in "tongues" during the services really freaked me out. I went anyway, though, and clapped and sang the hymns and pretended it wasn't the last place on earth that I wanted to be.

My girlfriend and I even got baptized together there, even though it wasn't until decades later that I actually understood that water baptism doesn't save anyone; it was merely an outward confession of our inner faith. The problem is that I hadn't received that inner faith in Christ yet, and I'm pretty sure my better half hadn't either, and although Pastor Sam soaked me pretty good in that pool, I doubt there was enough water in all of Burlington to wash away the sin that had taken root within my soul, but even that didn't matter very much.

My love and I were together, in each other's company, and every person in that church could have been screaming Hail Marys, and we wouldn't have noticed. We were truly young and in love, and nothing else in the world mattered.

We knew almost from our first date that we were soulmates and that one day we'd be husband and wife.

When we announced our engagement, everybody and their uncle expressed their lack of faith in our getting married at such young ages (she was eighteen, and I was twenty-one), but little did they know that their lack of faith and support actually helped to draw us even closer together. It embodied an "us against the world" chip on our shoulders. Unlike many of our contemporaries who were getting married and divorced within a year, we were very determined to keep our vows. That really wouldn't be much of a challenge, however, since we were the real deal. We were in love from that starstruck moment at the McDonald's counter.

Pastor Sam

Pastor Sam was a very intimidating old-school Italian Pentecostal hell-and-damnation preacher, to say the least. I remember when we had to meet with him at his church office to discuss the responsibilities of marriage prior to him agreeing to do the service. I was shaking in my boots during that meeting, hoping that he couldn't see that I wasn't the innocent choirboy type that I had been pretending to be. Although I certainly wasn't a "ten" on the addict/alcoholic scale any longer, I also would not have been able to pass a drug test if he had required one.

As it turned out, he agreed to marry us anyway, most likely because he was good friends with the my fiancée's dad, and Italians are loyal to each other . . . you know . . . the old Pizon "de familia" thing.

One of the Best Days of My Life

On September 4, 1982, we tied the knot. Our wedding was like a dream. It was a beautiful sunny fall day in Mount Holly. We were joined in matrimony by Pastor Sam at the First Christian Assembly Pentecostal church on Main Street in Burlington, New Jersey. My bride's family spared no expense for us. We had a huge bridal party consisting of six bridesmaids adorned in stunning violet silk gowns, along with six groomsmen decked out in designer black-and-white tuxedos. There was a guest singer as well as the absolutely amazing Suzuki violinists.

Is there anything in this world that compares to the excitement a groom experiences while awaiting to witness the beauty of his bride-to-be upon entering the church to take his hand in matrimony? There has certainly never been anything that approaches that feeling to me except for the feeling of bearing children with that very same bride. The excitement was completely justified.

As I stood alongside my brother (my best man) and the groomsmen, along with a completely filled church, awaiting her entrance, I can remember an amazing calm that was poured over me as the events proceeded in slow motion. A red carpet was rolled out, the sanctuary door opened, and I watched as my bride's father entered with what can only be described as an angel on his arm. As he was softly shedding the tears of a man about to lose his most precious treasure, it appeared as if they were floating toward me as I attempted to breathe while absorbing the glamour of the angel's pearl-covered wedding gown.

When she was finally beside me, her father lifted the veil off her face to reveal the most beautiful woman my eyes had surely ever seen. She could only be described as glowing. Her face was perfectly made up as if she were a porcelain doll. There was no detail left undone, perfection. Even her eyeshadow matched the color of the bridesmaids' gowns. They say there has only been one perfect person to ever walk the face of the earth, but seeing what I saw when that veil was lifted, I beg to differ.

The entire service was majestic, followed by an equally perfect reception, which was held in her family's always immaculately landscaped backyard. They personally catered the entire buffet-style event. You name it, we had it. There was ham, turkey, pork, beef, Italian manicotti with all the trimmings, and an entire table of every dessert imaginable. The food was out of this world!

A couple of months before the wedding, her father, who was always very handy, built a beautiful gazebo in the middle of their backyard. We knew it had some purpose in the wedding, but it was to be our surprise.

Following the ceremony, our families and the wedding party were driven by a procession of limousines to a beautiful lake nearby for wedding pictures that, because of their sheer beauty, most would believe were paintings.

Then came the big surprise. When we returned to her family's house for dinner, we were ushered through a side gate into a backyard filled with standing cheering guests. The gazebo was so romantically arranged that it can't be described. We had our own candlelit glass table for two, fitted with the finest chinaware, silverware, and crystal glasses.

The entire day was almost dreamlike. The excitement had consumed several hours yet was so tranquil that it seemed like a mere moment. The yard was filled to capacity with hundreds of quests, yet we were truly all alone in that gazebo while gazing into each other's eyes. We were special, and we knew it, and more than a few of the guests complimented that it was the most beautiful wedding they had ever experienced.

We borrowed my parents' Chevy Chevette to head to Florida for our honeymoon, although the journey ended once we reached contentment along the shores of Virginia Beach. We spent an entire two weeks there in pure newlywed bliss. No one really knows what heaven will be like, but if it's anything closely resembling those two weeks in Virginia, then the saints have quite a treat in store.

God's Word says that "He is able to do exceedingly abundantly above all that we ask or think . . ." (Eph. 3:20). Well, ain't that the truth?

Upon returning to New Jersey, the blessings continued. We had been offered a one-bedroom, two-bathroom apartment located on the second floor of the house that doubled as the management office for the owner of the same McDonald's who had united my wife-to-be and me. We would be permitted to live there rent-free, with one stipulation. We were responsible for our portion of the utilities bill and had to tend to all the property's needs (maintaining the exterior grounds and keeping the offices clean, vacuuming, trash removal, etc.). It didn't take a rocket scientist to recognize a win-win proposal. We gladly and thankfully accepted, and our journey to marital bliss had begun.

Living for free was short-lived, however. For the first time in our young joint-hood, we experienced the definition of trials and tribulations. Approximately 1-1/2 years into our extended honeymoon, the owner decided he didn't like my janitorial skills and requested that we move on. I wasn't emptying the trash or vacuuming any differently, so I could only suspect that he didn't enjoy the smell of marijuana smoke that radiated down from our second-floor penthouse to the his first-floor company board meetings. Who knows for sure, but one thing was for sure, I was beginning to slide back into that dark place that seems to follow people like me like dirt follows a pigpen. My wife began to take notice of it and made subtle suggestions that it would be in our best interests to cut out the partying aspect of my life.

First-Time Homeowners

With some much-needed help from my grandmother Bird, we saved up enough money to make a down payment on our first home. It was in the wonderfully secluded wooded section of Lumberton, New Jersey, called Sunnybrook. My brother and his wife had purchased a townhome there shortly before, as did my wife's sister and her husband, so that was good-enough confirmation for us. We were fortunate enough to buy a two-bedroom, two-bathroom end unit on one of the prime lots in the development. Although I have never believed in luck, it was becoming evident to us both, as well as anyone acquainted with us, that we could step in dog doo-doo and always come out smelling like roses.

In early 1986, with my wife firmly rooted in her position at a local bank and myself progressing well in the business world at Consarc, we decided it was time for our family to grow. We had been together for nearly six years and truly enjoyed our freedom, but it was time for the next stage of our lives, and we were very excited about it.

When it was acknowledged that she was carrying our first child, we were both overwhelmingly radiant and elated with the prospect of parenthood.

I quickly began wallpapering, painting, and decorating the baby's room, and we began shopping for a crib and furniture. As it would turn out, we had started the preparation a bit early, and our excitement was premature as well.

Before our baby-to-be had reached the completion of her first trimester, we suffered a miscarriage. The loss of our first baby was devastating. It was the worst day of our young relationship and very possibly the worst of our entire lives as a couple.

I'm not sure if it was the emptiness related to the disappointment of losing our first child or the boredom from the everyday weed and beer high, but my experimental juices had again been triggered after lying dormant for half a decade. Certainly, something must have crossed one of my wires to risk jeopardizing my career, my marriage, and even my life. Was it possible that maybe I was just an immature kid who wasn't prepared to wear his big boy panties quite yet?

I had been married and out on my own for over four years, yet I still wasn't ready to leave childhood and its security for adulthood and its corresponding responsibilities. Did I really want to remain in a sandbox, or was there some other underlining flaw that kept me bound to a state of puberty? Whatever was the excuse this time, it could never have justified entering the territory that I was about to explore.

The Iceman Cometh

My wife and I were crazy in love with one another, and although we had suffered a setback, our future remained filled with hopes and dreams. There was nothing on God's green earth strong enough to separate us from the love we had for each other. However, the "Iceman" certainly did not come from God and was never intended to be played with by children.

I have no idea how, where, or why it started, and there is no possible reasoning behind it, but like marijuana, alcohol, and everything else I had experimented with, I fell in love with cocaine, or "ice," from the very first "hit." I had tried a line of "crank" (rock form of amphetamine) from my weed dealer, which renewed a facsimile of the energy boost I had received from black beauties during my Blue Hen days. That one little line was all that was required to get my mind's experimental juices kick-started once again.

During the mid-eighties, cocaine had burst upon the scene in a major way. It was pretty much everywhere. I experimented with a twenty-five-dollar bag and, as usual, was instantly its biggest fan. One toothpick-sized line sent my euphoria modes into orbit.

Everything that a person could possibly do seemed to be so much more enjoyable on cocaine, whether it was performing at work, playing Yahtzee, or having sex. It not only made a person sharper and more alert, but it also made the simplest things like having a conversation a complete adventure. Whenever I was lucky enough to get my wife and some friends to join me in a round of lines, we'd sit and gossip well into the night and often right into the morning. It was amazing!

Truly the "8th Wonder of the World," we all thought . . . or should I say, I thought?

I wasn't the only one who was captivated by its taste and benefits. I learned quickly that many of my "pothead" friends also enjoyed a "bump" on occasion, with the only difference being that I had the hookup.

As they began getting hooked on the stuff just as I was, they relied on me to supply them. Before I knew it, I went from splitting a hundred-dollar bag amongst three or four of us to purchasing a couple of kilos a week. I was becoming a regular *Scarface*. It wasn't unusual for me to profit over $1000 in a weekend, and considering the low-paying careers we both had, that was a substantial amount of cash. The money was coming in so fast that I began contemplating quitting my legitimate full-time job to become a full-time dope dealer. Boy, what an aspiration for a twenty-five-year-old.

Before I could give Consarc my two weeks' notice, a problem arose. The "Iceman" had now taken complete ownership of my soul, and I was now snorting more product than I was selling, and I was selling a lot.

Nearly a year after the miscarriage, my wife was again with child. This time, except for my partying, we proceeded with caution. We both recognized the vital importance of parenting and discussed how we needed to make some changes in our lifestyle prior to the arrival of our new addition. It certainly made perfect sense, and she made the change, which was the responsible thing to do; however, I wasn't prepared to face responsibility just yet.

Parenthood

Our first perfect son, David Scott Gaskill Jr., or D.J., as we called him, was born on 5/17/87, followed by our second son Adam Alexander on 9/10/1991. It was an absolutely amazing time in our lives, and we cherished every single moment of it, from the Jersey shore vacations to the 4th of July fireworks at Milldam Park to walks at the mall. Yet, even the joy of waking up every three hours in the middle of the night to feed and change D.J.'s "load" still wasn't quite the awakening needed to spur me into adulthood. Actually, it was quite the contrary. I used the 3:00 a.m. feedings as an opportunity to not only receive brownie points for "Father of the Year" but also a stepping stone for "Cokehead of the Year."

Yet, even as high as I was at times, I could still see D.J.'s content face as he inhaled a bottle in my arms while gazing wondrously into my eyes. I could hear his subtle burps and smell the corresponding fragrance of formula as it filled the air. Those were truly absurdly magical moments for me.

The Trip of All Trips

What should have been some of the most special times of our young family's life nearly tragically ended on one horrid weekend.

My wife was off at work on a Saturday morning, D.J. was at her parents', and I was home alone. For me, being alone was never a good thing. My wife, knowing that my habit and I could not be trusted, had begun hiding my coke supply so that it wouldn't go up my nose before I could sell it. It was a perfectly good strategy except that it is not possible to hide drugs from a drug addict. It's as if we have a sixth sense, almost like a bloodhound has for sniffing out a bird. We can sniff out drugs with our eyes closed, if need be, to satisfy our intense thirst for personal gratification.

I quickly located the stash under the storage cabinet in our laundry room, and the party was on. The days of enjoying TV shows, Yahtzee, and any other harmless activity at a quicker, more exhilarating pace was completely erased by the desire to enter another realm of consciousness. Whether the realm I was seeking was heaven or not didn't matter on this weekend. I was on a one-way ticket to hell, and there was no one there to stop me.

After a couple of hours of nonstop snorting, I completely snapped. A horrible demonic paranoia was kicking in, and knowing that my wife would be home soon, I had to exit stage left quickly.

I picked up the bag of coke and hopped into my car. I had no idea where I was going. I just knew that I wasn't ready for the party to be over just yet. After all, I was an addict and still had a half-ounce of blow left. I couldn't stop; I was powerless, and there just was no way.

I stopped at a liquor store and grabbed a pint of Southern Comfort and then found myself in a motel room with the lights turned off, the curtains drawn, and the bed pushed up against the door to fend off the police, FBI, or whoever else might be following me.

I then proceeded to spend the rest of the afternoon snorting lines on the floor and bouncing up and down from there to the bathroom window to the front window and back to the floor at a frenetic pace while filled with the terror that I was being watched. I was sweating profusely as this continued on until the sun began setting.

I finally called my wife from the hotel phone to somehow explain my disappearance. I told her that I "just had to get away." I just wanted to be alone. "Everything is okay. I'll be home in a little while," I assured her.

She kept pleading with me. "Where are you, Dave? What are you doing? Let me come and get you!"

I could feel the fear in her voice as she continued to try and talk sense to me, but all I could say was, "I'm at a hotel, and I'll be home soon," and then I hung up.

She had witnessed many of my two-to-three day binges, but this one was different. I had never holed myself up in a hotel room before. Something very scary was going on, and we both knew it. I had become a full-fledged monster on this Saturday afternoon, completely out of control of rational thinking or behavior.

As I began running out of the half-ounce of cocaine that I had set off with, and knowing the withdrawal pain I was heading for if I did, I began plotting on how to replenish it. I first had to go home and get some money, which also meant confronting my wife. That somehow didn't seem like an obstacle to me, however. I would zip in, grab whatever money I could find, then zip out without answering any of her questions, almost as if I was invisible—weird, since I had just spent six-to-eight hours trying to hide from imaginary agents and was now somehow believing she wouldn't even see me sneaking in and out of our house.

When I arrived home, much to my joy, I found my wife's sister there, but my wife was nowhere to be found. She had gone to her parents to pick up D.J., she said. I immediately began pestering her for coke. "Do you know anybody who has a little? I just need a little to help me 'come down.'" Coming down from a minor binge, if there is such a thing, is brutal, but what I was facing at the end of this major ride could be fatal.

She went into the next room and called my wife to inform her that I was there and okay. Then, to stall my badgering, she tried to convince me that my wife was going to bring me home a couple of grams. I was so relieved, but the longer I waited for her, the clearer it became that they had merely conspired together to keep me there.

I took off out of the house and headed to nowhere in particular to find some coke. It was early evening by now, and I was beginning to withdraw and was desperate. I pulled up at a stoplight, and while sitting there sweating, my brother pulled up next to me. What were the odds that he'd find me sitting there in the dark? Divine intervention? Possibly, but I wasn't listening to reasoning at that point.

He began honking his horn and rolled down his window and yelled, "Dave, I love you! Please follow me! Your wife and everybody are over at her parents' house (a short drive away) and scared to death!"

All I said was, "I love you too," and sped through the red light like I was fleeing the police and drove 100 mph, leaving my dear brother with no chance of catching me.

I located some coke at a bar that night to stop the comedown (withdraw) and then finally headed home. When I got there, I was pleased that I didn't see my wife's car there; however, I again walked into a surprise. When I entered my house, my brother was sitting on the couch waiting for me. He was relieved to see me, and all he said was, "Are you okay?" I nodded yes with my head down, too ashamed to look at him, and headed into my bedroom, shut the door, and finished off the blow before passing out.

My wife, who arrived home the next morning alone, said she left D.J. at her parents' house. My mom arrived as well. I can't even imagine the fear and anguish I had put the two women who loved me the most through.

My wife went straight to the bedroom, grabbed a suitcase, and quickly began packing her stuff. She said, "I'm done! That's it. I'm outta here!" I was crying and begging her to stay, and so was my mom. She started crying, and I hugged her and sincerely promised that I'd stop using cocaine if she'd give me one more chance. She put the bag down and stayed.

A day that started with me and a half-ounce of cocaine alone in a run-down hotel room and culminated with a high-speed car chase between my brother and me had literally brought both the Gaskills and my wife's family to their knees. When I came to, and the dust had settled, I had come within a hair of losing my spouse and visiting hell, once and for all.

I kept my word and sent the Iceman away . . . for a season.

The Fear Factor

Addicts look for excuses to get high and create them when they can't find any. I believe that fear was a major influence in my escalation in substance abuse. Soon after deserting my secret Friend, it started. First, it was the fear of dropping out of school and the unknown that would follow that decision. Then later, early in our marriage, there were many fears. I had gotten married at twenty-one years of age and certainly was a man only by the date on my birth certificate.

My parents did an amazing job of protecting me from the evils of the world; however, unbeknownst to them or me at the time, it thwarted my maturity development. Even until this day, it appears that I am frozen in the seventeen to nineteen-year-old mindset, which certainly has its pros but was a major con for a young man who was trusted to protect and provide for his wife and children.

I wasn't willing to share my cowardliness with anyone except my secret Friend, but after deserting Him in Henry's dormitory room in 1979, I only pulled out my ace in the hole during the most extreme of circumstances.

"What if I lose my job? I don't have a degree, so how will I find work? How will I be able to take care of my wife?" That fear grew as our children were born, the fear of becoming unemployed and my family having to live on the streets. Then, as I grew older, I began fearing that my wife would leave me or something would happen to my beloved children. All the fears were unfounded as I continued to get promoted at work, and so did my wife. I also had health fears because of the way I abused my body. I feared cancer from all the substances I was pumping into my once self-proclaimed temple. I was afraid of reality and the world, along with its responsibilities. I wanted and needed to escape, and my addictions grew in direct correlation with my fears.

A New Drug of Choice

By the early 1990s, I was already a full-fledged drunk or "functional alcoholic", as it's referred to in AA since I continued to work full time and later coached or assisted on all my sons' baseball, basketball, and football teams. I was able to pretty much keep my demons hidden from nearly everyone outside of my house.

In 1994, my body and my life began to fail me. I first came down with diabetes, then a couple of years later, in January 1995, I suffered a back injury that ignited a chain of events, which led to my ultimate doom as well as my beloved family's.

I was lifting a box containing our artificial Christmas tree up into our attic when I felt what I can only describe as an explosion inside my mid-section. It knocked me to the floor and momentarily paralyzed me. I lay there prone on my back for quite a while. When I was able to get to my feet, I realized I had no feeling in my left leg or foot. The diagnosis was two herniated disks (L4, L5) in my lower back. I was prescribed Vicodin, which was a high I never experienced before.

I had a laminectomy and was doing pretty well until I blew out my back again in 2001 shoveling dirt while landscaping our new inground pool at our newly built custom home in the Oxmead Crossing section of Burlington Township, New Jersey. I blew out the same two disks and was diagnosed with spinal stenosis and degenerative disk disease.

This time, I was sent to a pain management doctor to try and manage the pain with injections and a higher dosage of pain meds, much to my delight.

The introduction of narcotic pain medications into my already addictive lifestyle consisting of booze and weed sent me hurtling into a deep dark hole, a black fog that there was no turning back from.

I immediately fell in love with any and all narcotics. It began with the "Vicodin ride," then climbed the stairway to narcotic heaven by playing the doctor into prescribing me Oxycontin (bootleg heroin) for long-term pain relief to go with ACTIQ fentanyl lollipops (generally prescribed for cancer-related pain) for short-term quick relief, or as it is termed, "breakthrough" pain.

I had read about Oxycontin on the internet, about the effects (the high) when crushing it and snorting it, and had no problem convincing my pain specialist that it was the only med that could relieve my chronic pain. After all, it was a fact that my back really was destroyed as my surgeon Dr. K had described it, and I also had developed a high tolerance for the narcotics and needed something stronger.

The problem with pain meds is that the more you take, the more you need to take. Yet, it was also a fact that I was still on an endless search for "it," the ultimate high, kind of like a surfer's quest for the perfect wave. It was out there for sure; I was certain of that, a place within me where I could find freedom from the spirit versus the flesh battle that was raging within me and had me feeling like a lion in a cage most of my life (Gal 5:17).

Although I had two major surgeries to fix my back, I only seemed to get worse. I could still feel a semblance of pain running down my leg, which justified the continued use of narcotics, at least that's what I had convinced myself, the doctors, and everyone else of.

My life became a wicked cycle of doctor visits, prescriptions, pharmacy visits, and then horrible overdoses month after month. The demon had his grips on me, and I had absolutely no control over his power.

I began seeing multiple doctors, getting multiple scripts, and going to multiple pharmacies. The opioid epidemic and all of its restrictions hadn't gone into effect until around 2010, so there was no database in place to track my sneaky yet brilliant behind.

I simply could not feed the demon enough pills, so I learned how to order Vicodin on the internet and had them shipped UPS to my office at Consarc, right to my desk. Yeah, I suppose you could say I was too smart for my own britches, as Mom used to say, although there was certainly nothing smart about my schemes.

The Beginning of the End

Certainly, my wife wasn't fooled. A few months before I was scheduled to have a radical procedure done (installation of a morphine pump into my abdomen to pump morphine directly into my spine), she convinced me to sell our home in Burlington Township. She wanted to move to Florida and "start our life over," as she put it. The past several years had taken a huge toll on us and our once perfect marriage.

Because of the progression of my addictive behavior and habits, I began looking at her differently. She had become an object to me, and I treated her as such. I became disgusting to her, and rightly so, and was reduced to begging for sex much like a kid for a toy at a grocery store, but instead of crying when I didn't succeed, the evil would come out of me, as she referred to it, and I'd lace her with obscenities, throw things, and punch holes in the walls of our house.

I had been so afraid of losing her since, in my heart, I didn't feel like I had deserved her in the first place. She was an amazing woman. She had a natural high. She was everything I wasn't. She had discipline, had her life in order, was under control, and was the rock of our family.

I, on the other hand, had become way out of shape, was rarely seen without a drink and a joint in my hand, and was frequently calling in sick to work. I had gone from being proud and thankful for having such an amazing wife to extremely jealous, controlling, verbally abusive, and blaming everything I possibly could on her.

Maybe a change of scenery would help, she explained to me. It was a very difficult decision. We both had lived our entire lives (she was forty-one, and I was forty-four at the time) within a five-to-ten-mile radius of Mount Holly, New Jersey, where both of our parents still lived.

Since I was still at Consarc after nearly twenty-four years and making good money for a college dropout with no degree to fall back on, I was very apprehensive, actually scared, at the prospect of finding employment down there. Probably the only thing that swayed my decision to sell our beautiful brand-new 5000 square-foot house in the woods was the fact that her beautiful big brown eyes owned me and that David Jr. had decided to attend the University of South Florida in Tampa, Florida, and I already missed him terribly.

Our house sold very quickly (within three to four months) and at the perfect height of the real estate boom of 2005, so the plan was that after the settlement, she'd move down to Florida into an apartment, start job searching (she had been in the banking industry over twenty years and, unlike myself, was very confident in finding employment), and get things set up while I'd stay in New Jersey temporarily, have my morphine pump surgery, then move down as soon as I was able.

It sounded like a plan, so I flew down to Tampa with my youngest son Adam to enroll him in eighth grade and begin practicing with the Hurricanes Pop Warner football team. He was loaded with talent and long aspired to be a University of Miami Hurricane quarterback one day. He would be staying at his uncle's house (my wife's youngest brother) until she arrived in a few weeks after we closed on our house.

When it was time for me to return to Jersey, leaving Adam at the Tampa airport was one of the most emotional moments of my life. I had always been deeply involved in every aspect of my sons' lives, whether it was helping them with homework, coaching their teams, attending parent-teacher conferences, taking them to doctor visits, or just being their friend. I was their hero, and they were my reason for living, and now both of them were about to be separated from my life.

When Adam hugged me tightly goodbye, the pain of leaving him, such an innocent, sweet young child , had me choking back tears. With his head slightly bowed, he quietly asked, "You'll be back soon, right?" Our sons weren't ignorant of their parents' indiscretions. Unfortunately, they had experienced some really nasty arguments between us, admittedly mostly instigated by myself, stemming from jealousy and unforgiveness. I optimistically answered, "I sure hope so, son," not knowing that it would be one year and two months before I'd move permanently down to Florida.

When I arrived back in New Jersey, my wife, her parents, and sister had most of the house packed, and within a couple of days, the settlement on it was completed, the moving trucks had been loaded, and I sent her on her way to Florida.

With my wife of nearly twenty-four years leaving and the future of our marriage as uncertain as the New Jersey weather, did my heart break? Did I crawl into a hole and cry like a newborn baby? No, not me! I was an alcoholic drug addict who had lost touch with emotions long, long ago. I was actually excited when she left. All I could think about was getting together with my bottle of 80 mg. Oxycontin pills. They were my wife now, my family, and had been for quite a while, so I headed to the liquor store, then to my apartment, promptly crushed up a couple, and snorted my way into oblivion.

Hoodwinked

Immediately before and after her departure, I learned things weren't going to go quite the way I had hoped and had been led to believe. My wife had been one busy little beaver, working behind the scenes and arranging for her new life, a life that did not include me.

She had already taken out a lease for a one-bedroom apartment for myself in Lumberton, New Jersey, as well as a two-bedroom condo for her and the kids in the Carrollwood section of Tampa, Florida. She had also closed out our joint bank accounts, opened separate accounts, and much like Bonnie Parker after a heist, I'd later be enlightened, left town with every penny we had, including over $200,000 from the sale of our home in Burlington Township.

Looking back, that may have been the wisest thing she had ever done because God knows my share of that money surely would have gone right up my nose like every other dime I had to my name. And although she deposited $5000 in my new account, I still felt like Moses when he had received only a ration of water from Pharaoh to help cross the desert wilderness.

When the smoke had cleared, and I called her soon after her departure, the tone in her voice had completely changed. They say, "Hell has no fury like a woman scorned," especially an Italian woman scorned; well, let's just say she simply had had enough. She was hurt and extremely angry. Our last few years up north had been a blur because of my daily consumption of alcohol, weed, and pain meds. I was like a zombie from *The Night of the Living Dead*: numb to the world and completely separated, not only from my best Friend, her, and my sons but everybody and everything else in mind, body, soul, and spirit.

She had given me an ultimatum a year or so back: "Make a choice . . . It's either me and the kids or your drugs."

Well, since I certainly couldn't or wouldn't exist without my "candy" and seriously doubted she'd ever leave me, her soulmate, anyway, I replied, "You can't wipe your a—— without me!" I guess that wasn't the most intelligent response to give to a Sicilian woman who had been scorned, was scared, and hurting terribly.

Much to my chagrin, she learned how to wipe her butt real quick. She told me, "This is your wake-up call!" She wouldn't even tell me where she had moved to. She said she didn't want me anywhere near my sons, that they had seen enough. Boy, was that the truth and a major understatement. God bless her for her strength and courage. Although I was not willing to accept it then, she was right.

The realization that my family, the only thing in this world that once mattered to me, my entire universe, my purpose for living, was gone finally hit me a few weeks later like a Mike Tyson uppercut to the jaw.

Our Family
Always Prospered

From the very first moment we met, our relationship was noticeably charmed. It always appeared as if the pieces to our ultimate destiny were coming together one at a time. Even though we persevered many pressing tests (first cocaine scare, miscarriage, an entanglement, my illnesses and injuries, alcoholism/addiction), much like a cat being thrown into the air, not only did we always end up landing on our feet, but our relationship also seemed to grow stronger by it.

Over the course of our careers, we both were promoted numerous times. She started as a minimum wage-earning McDonald's waitress, then moved to the banking industry and worked her way up from a teller to a branch manager while being employed at the same bank for nearly twenty years. I began as a minimum wage-earning grill master at the same burger joint, prospered to another minimum wage position as a shipping clerk at Consarc, and eventually was promoted to the salaried position of After Market Sales Manager for over a period of twenty-four years of employment.

We first lived in the one-bedroom apartment above the McDonald's office (1982), then purchased our first home, a two-bedroom, two-bathroom townhouse in Sunnybrook (1985), graduated to a four-bedroom single family home in Edgewater Park (1992), then to our dream home in Burlington Township (2001).

I doubt either of us ever recognized then that each house that we sold became the highest-selling house in their respective neighborhoods. Although we had a small return on the Edgewater Park property based on the declining neighborhood conditions, we more than made up for it by doubling each of our original investments on the Lumberton and Burlington houses.

We both began our automobile driving careers with the typical hand-me-down specials. I purchased an old Chevy Belair for $200, while my wife saved up enough money during her McDonald's days to splurge $1500 on a luxurious Chrysler Buick New Yorker Brougham. We were able to rock our first new car, a Toyota Cavalier, only a couple of years into our marriage. We began purchasing a new car every couple of years and eventually progressed to the point where we each had new cars.

Our vacations also progressed up the prosperity ladder in direct correlation to our careers, houses, and automobiles. Following our first vacation (honeymoon) to the shores of Virginia Beach, we began going on yearly beach vacations to the New Jersey and Maryland shores. Sandwiched in between were four trips to the Florida amusement parks (Disney and Universal Studios) as well as at least a half dozen Pocono Mountain winter ski trips.

Then, after my wife and I fell in love with the turquoise waters and white sandy beaches of the Bahamas, we began exploring the Caribbean Islands each year: Jamaica (twice), St. Thomas (twice), Saint John, Virgin Gorda, Cozumel, Punta Cana, and capped off by our last vacation as a family to Riviera Maya.

Twenty-four years of vacations, and never, not even once, was the weather anything but perfect. It was uncanny! It was almost as if a cloud of blessings followed us no matter where we went or what we did. But even more interestingly, it appeared as if the cloud of blessings was actually following closely behind the cloud of curses.

My addictions and destructive behavior were also prospering in proportion to our material prosperity. Even my own evil couldn't manage to run away from or be separated from the goodness of God that always covered us like a blanket. Even though we were going to church three times a week at the onset of our marriage, then twice a week, then once a week, then not at all, God kept blessing us. The goodness of God is based on His goodness and grace, not ours.

Do you think we ever gave Him any credit? Oh no . . . it was all because we were intelligent, ambitious, and hard-working, and we were just receiving the fruits of our labor. It was all because of us. . . What did we need God for anymore? We had everything.

"Pride goes before destruction, and a haughty spirit before a fall" (Prov. 16:18). Surely, the fall was coming.

The Morphine Pump

had outpatient surgery to install the morphine pain pump into my abdomen. The plan was to stay at my parents' house a couple of days to recover, but instead, I got into an argument with my mother when she sensed me being high, which I took offense to, even though I was (I received a prescription for Percocet following the surgery), and I demanded her to drive me to my apartment to recover instead.

Since I now had the pain pump, the doctor wouldn't prescribe me anymore pain meds. What? How was I going to numb the pain, the unbearable pain that rules every addict? The mental, as well as often physical pain of a constant "war within" the soul? The constant fear of facing reality? A spirit locked in total darkness, yearning so desperately to see the "light"? The pain that sometimes feels like it's going to literally rip you in two? It was the physical, mental, and spiritual pain that ONLY an addict can relate to.

Although the pump was still pumping me full of morphine, it was regulated by a computer chip, so I had NO control over how much it gave me or when it gave it. There was no "high" from it. Darn it! I was hoping it was like the ones in the hospital where you just push the red button anytime you needed a "fix." Man, was I wrong. I would have never agreed to have had it installed if I had known this. There's no way to overdose with the pump . . . believe me, I tried everything! I tried covering it with a heating pad, hoping heat would release the morphine faster like it did with the narcotic fentanyl patches I was once on. And although the pump was installed in my belly, I tried my darnedest to get it to release more morphine by pressing on the rubber button that was on the top of the pump itself, the place where the doc refilled the morphine.

Good Lord, my world was caving in on me! The world that I had been afraid to face most of my adult life, I was now forced to face alone. You see, I had never been afraid of dying from the astronomical amounts of drugs and alcohol I consumed. I was Superman, as my wife so often referred to me; I was afraid of living. Horrified of it! I couldn't fall asleep at night, and even when I'd pass out from the booze or pills, it would only afford me brief "cat naps." I'd sometimes go days without sleep, and if and when I did nod off, I'd break out in cold sweats, fearing the coming of the next day. I went years without really experiencing a good night's sleep.

The thought that my wife may be gone forever absolutely terrified me. Here I had been trying to control almost every aspect of her life for years, when, in fact, she had been the one controlling my life. She was my glue. She was the only one I could go to. I counted on her alone. She had become my replacement for my once best Friend. I had isolated myself so far from my family and friends that I truly had no one but her. She was it, and now she was gone. Was this really happening, or would I wake up after a night of hallucinating from an Oxycontin overdose and find out it was just a terrible nightmare? Nah, it was real as a heart attack.

Talk about a Binge

My depression grew almost by the minute and took my drinking to a new level, which, to most human beings, wouldn't seem possible. I began drinking a 1.75-liter bottle of rum or vodka almost daily. My primary doctor, Dr. Murray Buck, had diagnosed me with bipolar disorder and manic depression, as well as insomnia, obsessive compulsive disorder, and anxiety deficit disorder. I'm sure I probably had a few other disorders, but at least we were off to a good start. He started prescribing me anti-depressants, anti-anxiety, as well as sleeping pills, and of course, I immediately began abusing all of them. The combination of the three mixed with booze and weed should have sent me for a sure dirt nap, but they didn't, so I drank and drank and drank.

I wasn't working at the time (I was on disability from the pump surgery), yet my employer of twenty-four years apparently decided they had had enough of my erratic and unreliable behavior and found a reason to send me a termination letter. Man, did that hurt. After twenty-four years of being overworked and underpaid, it ended with a FedEx letter delivered on a Saturday morning.

What a roll I was on, huh? In less than two months, my family, house, and now job were all gone. Could anything possibly stop the bleeding? Well, I was soon going to find out.

I headed straight to the liquor store to find solace and began a binge unlike any other. I honestly wasn't trying to die; I was just determined not to wake up (does that make any sense at all?). I began with my normal drink of about 3/4 of a 24-oz. glass filled with rum mixed with a splash of Diet Coke. Each day, I'd drive to the liquor store across the street and get another bottle.

After about three days of constant drinking with minimal sleep (I'd only nod off for a few hours periodically with the help of a handful of pills, then return to the bottle), I began losing touch with reality. Duh, ya think!

At one point, when I got in my car to go fetch another bottle, and believe me, driving was becoming more and more of a major problem with each trip, I noticed it was extremely dark. Possibly, a storm was coming. When I got to the store, I noticed the parking lot was empty, but it only hit me that they may be possibly closed for a holiday when I got to the store door and found it to be locked. What to do? Nothing I could do, so I weaved my way back home and staggered into my apartment. Only then when I turned my TV on did I realize it was 4 a.m. Duh! No wonder the store was closed. No problem. I took a nap for a few hours, then returned to the store to replenish my supply as soon as it opened.

This cycle continued for about a week until one day, my oldest son David called. He informed me that my mom was on her way to my apartment. "What for?" I yelled at him. He said it was because no one had been able to get in touch with me for a week. My wife had been calling, as well as my mother, with no answer, and they feared for my life, knowing the state of depression I had fallen into.

Before I could hang up the phone, the police knocked my door down. There stood my parents, horrified at the sight of me. My mom looked like she was in shock. She was crying and screaming at me at the same time. "No wonder she left you!"

My father ran to me, crying profusely, and hugged me like he had never hugged me before. He kept repeating, "I love you, David. I love you!" as tears poured down his face. It may have been the first time in my life that I remember him doing either of those two things, although I'm sure he probably had.

I could barely stand and hadn't eaten, showered, shaved, or changed my clothes in well over a week. The two police officers helped carry me to my parents' car. They quickly raced me to my doctor's office about a mile away. I remember my mom saying she ran through the front door to the desk and begged the lady was there. "Please help my son!"

After giving her the particulars of my condition, the lady told my mom to take me straight to a hospital in Cherry Hill (about fifteen minutes away), which specializes in overdoses. Man, I never saw my dad drive so fast! They rushed me in the door, and the staff quickly took over. I don't remember exactly what my blood alcohol content was (close to .30, I believe), but I remember the doctor telling my parents that if they hadn't gotten me there so quickly, I would have been dead in an hour.

They did further testing, which revealed I had a pulmonary embolism (blood clots in my lungs) caused by the fact that I had been lying on my back prone, drinking constantly, and rarely getting up for the entire week, causing blood to settle in my lungs. I was in real bad shape, to say the least.

I had had many close calls over the previous twenty-four years of playing Russian Roulette and having overdosed well over a hundred times from narcotics, but this ranked way up on the screw-up list for sure.

My son David even flew up from Florida out of concern for me, but the sight of his pop strapped to the bed (to prevent the clots from releasing to my heart and brain) with IV lines was heartbreaking, even to a young man mature well beyond his eighteen years. He had seen me messed up many times before but never hospitalized for it.

I remember when he and his girlfriend Krystallo walked into my room. David took one look at me, then quickly took an about-face and walked out. When they returned a couple of minutes later, David was wiping away tears and was too hurt to even look up at me. I repeated to him, "It'll be okay, son; it'll be okay," but in my heart, and maybe for the first time, it actually hit me that my self-destructive behavior was hurting everyone in my family, probably even more so than myself.

First, seeing my mom and dad crying, and now D.J., man oh man, what was I doing? This truly should have and would have been my last hurrah if an "angel of the Lord" hadn't saved me, or should I say angels? Psalm 91:11 says, "For He will give His angels charge over you, to keep you in all your ways."

Thank You, Lord, for sending me angels. My son, my wife, my parents, the police, and the mysterious lady at the front desk at my doctor's office were all truly angels. Oh yea, that lady at the front desk . . . My mother later revealed to me that she returned to thank her a few days later, only to be informed by the staff that no one existed at that office who even remotely fit the description of the lady my mother spoke with, the lady who ultimately had saved my life. Yes, you better believe God sends His angels to protect us.

My wife called me in the hospital upon hearing about the severity of my condition. She was scared and said she was going to fly up to see me; however, I was in no state of mind to see her or anyone else. The fact that I was still alive, unemployed, that her and my beloved sons were gone, and that I was forced to face my demons and the train wreck called my life alone had me even more depressed, extremely confused, hurt, and angry.

I barked at her, "Oh, now you wanna see me when a month ago you wouldn't even tell me where you were!"

She had completely misled me and desperately fled to start a new life without me. She was crying (I was always good at making her do that) and, in her defense, explained, "I was hurt! I didn't know what else to do!"

She said she didn't want anything to happen to me, that I was her soulmate. In an effort to cheer me up, I suppose, she said that I was Superman, that I couldn't die, and that I was gonna outlive them all, basing that statement on the fact that I had overdosed literally hundred times and was still alive to talk about it.

I must admit, though, her call touched me and restored in me some hope for us. Maybe she truly loved me after all, who knows?

Suddenly, I didn't wanna die anymore. I wanted to work things out, somehow, someway. Maybe something good was gonna come out of this after all.

I Wanted and Needed Help

The severity of this entire incident, the hurt on D.J.'s face, and the fact that I really didn't want to leave my kids without a father, along with my mother's scolding, inspired me to finally seek help for my problem. I called every alcohol/addiction program and inpatient and outpatient program that I could find in the phone book. I truly did want to finally end the bondage, the darkness, the war within, that I had been fighting and losing for twenty-eight years. I wanted my family back. I almost even wanted to live.

However, wouldn't you know, none of the programs would accept my insurance or were way too expensive for me to afford. So I was again alone to fight the beast.

After my release from the hospital, I had to continue on a daily regime of blood thinners, along with blood tests several times a week in an effort to regulate my blood count to the proper level. Oh yea, I was also told, "No more drinking!"

Well, my abstinence from booze lasted about two days before I returned to my bad habits all over again. I just couldn't stay sober. I didn't know how to face the "light" after living in "darkness" all those years. I didn't know how to "just say no" to myself, to my own evil desires. I couldn't do it when I had my family to come home to, and now without them, I was just totally defenseless. That was until one special visit to Dr. Buck. I'll never forget that day.

I was in a room waiting for him, and when he entered, I knew I was in deep "doo-doo." He was pissed at me! He said, "You have two options, David. Number one, you can bleed to death from the blood thinners, or number two, you can have a clot go to your heart or brain and die that way. So, which one is it?"

As always, being the smart ass that I was, I wisecracked, "What's option three?"

He wasn't laughing. He said, "Your blood sugar is way outta control! Your cholesterol is over 1000! The highest we've ever seen! Your blood pressure is off the charts! You're a stroke waiting to happen! If you drink again, you're gonna die! So what's it gonna be?"

I was truly touched by the sincerity of his overall concern for my health, my life. I agreed to stop drinking, and I did, for a season.

Physical Fitness: My New High

I joined a gym close to my apartment and began working out daily. Like everything else in my life, my weight had also been way outta control for quite a while due to my weed smoking, excessive drinking, and the associated uncontrollable munchies. I had ballooned to nearly 300 lbs., up from my wedding day weight of 185. I was one fat hog, yet I didn't feel fat and thought I only looked fat on our home and vacation videos, like that made any sense either. In hindsight, very little of what I was thinking or had been doing at the time made much sense for that matter.

I started a walking routine on the treadmill at the gym, and to my surprise, the weight began to quickly melt off. Then, I also incorporated a weight-lifting program.

One day while lifting, I met a young man at the gym who was huge. He was a body builder training for Mr. Teen USA and certainly looked the part. As we got to know each other, he divulged his secret, like I didn't already know. He was on the "juice" (steroids).

Being once addicted to steroids in my late twenties, I was well aware of the juice and its effects. I had gotten huge myself (54" chest, 32" waist, and 21" biceps), as well as freakishly strong (my bench press went from less than 200 lbs. to close to 400 lbs. within a yr.) from a combination of pills and daily injections of testosterone. I had only quit using them when I developed painful cysts in my kidneys, as well as "bitch tits" (fatty tissue that causes swelling around the nipples). But now, about fifteen years later and sober, except for weed, I was again thirsty for a steroid high.

It's funny how time had taken away the fear that had stopped me from using them in the first place. It wasn't funny, though, as most addicts learn, and just as the Bible teaches in Matthew 12:43–45, when you clean up your act and quit drinking or using drugs, the devil leaves you for a while, then when you return to them, the demon attacks you seven times harder, and so was the case with my new juice obsession. Muscles do have memory, and I was quickly getting big again.

Mr. USA was supplying me until I learned how to order whatever I wanted over the internet and have them delivered right to my mailbox. Amazing! Modern technology.

Time to Reconcile

Things were looking up. I began taking trips down to Florida every month or so, and all were noticing the difference in me. For the first time in many years, I actually cared about my looks. First and foremost, I wanted my wife back. I was in shape, had a nice tanning salon tan, was looking good and feeling good, physically, mentally, even a bit spiritually, was alcohol-free, and had an overall good countenance about myself.

My wife, although understandably guarded, was seemingly impressed. Her parents, who lived close by in New Jersey, on a stealth mission out of suspicion, I suppose, invited me out to dinner to check out the new me. I believe even they left impressed and were jumping on the bandwagon.

I wasn't working at the time. I went from receiving disability income from the surgery, then once that ran out, I started receiving unemployment income. I was barely getting by but really didn't care to work again. I enjoyed doing absolutely nothing but walking my dog Teddy, smoking a joint, and getting in an hour workout, day in and day out. I considered myself retired and was living as such.

I applied for Social Security disability and hired a lawyer on a contingency basis to handle my case. After all, I had five to six of the illnesses and injuries required to be approved: manic depression, bipolar, insomnia, ADD, OCD, and diabetes, as well as chronic back pain from spinal stenosis and degenerative disc disease. I recall my wife saying, "If anyone deserves it, it's you."

I'm not sure if I let them in on the worst problem of them all. I was a horrible addict/alcoholic with severe suicidal tendencies. Deep inside my soul, I had given up on myself, on this life, and the prospect of ever finding what my soul was searching for, aching for, that "it."

Although looking and feeling better physically, I was losing the fight mentally and spiritually. I had pretty much quit on myself and my best Friend. No, correction, I had quit.

The dream that my wife and I had shared for pretty much all of our marriage was to retire together, live in a house on the beach, and spend our days taking walks along the water, old and grey-haired, and happy was a distant memory now.

The Check

Right before my unemployment checks ran out, I received a big fat check from Consarc Corp. from my retirement plan. $220,000.00, and it was mine! This certainly would hold me over until I received another big fat retroactive check from my Social Security disability claim.

I began living like Charlie Sheen. I considered myself married as long as I was in the company of my wife in Florida, but while I was all alone up in Jersey, I considered myself free as a jaybird. Out of sight, out of mind, so to speak. After all, my estranged wife had stopped wearing her wedding ring months ago and informed me that she hadn't felt married in years. Boy, did that hurt. She might as well have put her picture up on one of the interstate billboards with the slogan, "I'm available!"

"Ok, fine," I said. Two can play at that game. In an effort to attract some strays, the wedding ring that I had cherished and had never taken off since the day my wife had first slid it onto my finger, I also began wearing less and less. I became a frequent guest at all the local "go-go" bars and clubs and pretty much ate out every meal. You would have thought I was a multi-millionaire judging by my prodigious living. The "prodigal son" that Jesus spoke about in Luke 15:11–32, that was me in waiting.

Although several months had gone by since my family had relocated, I was still very much stuck in quicksand in Jersey, with no real strong intentions of leaving. In my heart, I was kinda hoping they would change their minds about Florida, get homesick, turn around, return to Jersey, and we'd live happily ever after. But like most of my adult life, I was living in a dream world, unable to cope with reality.

She Was Our Rock

It was during one of my trips down to Florida early in the summer of 2006 to visit my wife and the kids that I was really taken back. Possibly for the first time, I was feeling her heart's conviction. We were taking a walk along Channelside Drive one beautiful sunny day and discussing our separation and marriage in general. I was trying to convince her that I had "turned the corner" regarding my problems and was asking her to give me another chance when she said, "You were my rock, my everything! But I'm my own rock now." She was right. She was my rock and our families rock as well.

Jesus had said, "The rains descended, the floods came, and the winds blew and beat on that house; and it fell. And great was its fall" (Matt. 7:27). He was referring to a man whose house had no foundation, a house built on sand instead of rock. If only I had become saved long ago and built the foundation of my life on the rock of Jesus Christ . . . if only.

In an effort to downplay the situation and get her to loosen up, I responded, "Come on, Rocky! Gimme another chance!" I laughed and attempted to hug her as she pulled away from me. In fact, she had refused to even hold hands with me during our walks or at any other time long, long ago. She was in no mood for my usual lack of seriousness concerning my addictions or our family's situation.

I pleaded, "Come on, don't do that! We can work this out. Gimme a chance! Give me until September to get saved! I can change! Just give me a chance to get saved." Why I chose September, I have no idea. Possibly, it was because September 4th was our anniversary, and it had always been such a special date for us, or maybe we could reconcile on our wedding day, or maybe I was just trying to buy a couple of more months. Who knows, but whatever the reason, she wasn't falling for my heartless promises anymore. It appeared that the days of her being conned were long gone.

She said, "Dave you're never going to change." Ironically, it had always been her pleading with me not to file for divorce, but now, as I continued begging, she uttered the prophetic words, "It would take a miracle for you to ever change." Who knew that she'd turn out to be a prophet.

I'm So Sorry, Son

Adam had called me in early September 2005. He wasn't enjoying football down there or anything else for that matter. They had moved him to running back, whereas, in Burlington Township, he had been an All-Star quarterback since he had begun playing as a six-year-old. He sounded so down, obviously so upset and confused by our whole family situation. He missed his friends up north, but most of all, he missed our family being together.

It was gut-wrenching. I missed my sweet sons so badly. Yet, I was terribly lost and couldn't even take care of myself. How was I going to take care of either of them?

I couldn't cook and certainly never liked to clean or do laundry. Let's face it, I was a slob. My wife was the one who always kept our house in order. All my job was to bring home a check, cut the grass, and coach the ball teams. I had it made and had a maid, so to speak.

It tore me up inside to tell my son, "No. I'm sorry, son, but you're much better off in Florida with your mom." It hurt so badly! And although I hadn't been able to feel much of anything emotionally for years, I sure as heck felt his pain, as well as my own.

He said, "I wanna come back home! I don't like Florida, and I don't want you to be all alone, Dad. Please, Dad! Let me come back home!"

Even being as cold and emotionless as I had allowed myself to become, my situation and my family's situation had become absolutely heartbreaking to all involved. However, Adam was the one who my selfishness had probably affected the most. Years later, as a sophomore at the University of South Florida (2012), he got together with a couple of friends and came out with a music "mix tape" entitled "Free

Interpretation." Two of the songs on the tape, "Someone" and "Adam and Evil," tore my soul. They were about the period when our family was still together but hanging by a thread. He described himself sitting upstairs in his room all alone, not being able to sleep, and contemplating suicide to get us to notice his pain. He felt ignored by us, maybe even insignificant.

The Kids Coming for the Summer

It was in the spring of 2006 that D.J. and Adam informed me they were coming up (to New Jersey) to stay with me once school let out for summer break. I was obviously very excited since I had only seen them for about a total of two weeks since they relocated to Florida the previous August.

Quite a bit had changed since then. I had been alcohol-free for about six months, and although I was still smoking a joint or so every day and shooting up the juice, I was a drastically different person.

Remember, I had denied Adam's effort to move in with me the previous September because of the sorry state I was in, but now I was anxiously looking forward to their visit.

D.J. would fly up in mid-May, with Adam to follow in June.

I remember my mother saying, "Maybe they'll wanna stay here once they've been here a couple of months." It was a possibility, but there was also a possibility I'd win the lottery, however remote the chances may have been.

Adam still had many ties to his friends in New Jersey and certainly must have been revisiting the memories of being the football, basketball, and baseball star he was when he left the previous summer, and of course, David remained crazy in love with his high school sweetheart Krystalo, just as he had been for many years.

God was offering me another big chance to make things right in my life and my family's, and I was very excited about it.

I dreamed that homesickness would draw my sons back to Jersey and thus prompt my wife to also return.

Why, Why, Why

Roughly about a month before D.J. was scheduled to arrive in New Jersey, I somehow allowed my guard to drop. "Idle hands are the devil's workshop," and except for going to the gym and taking Teddy for walks, I was bored as a betta fish in a fish bowl and made one of the worst choices in the history of idiotic choices.

The morphine pump had been doing a satisfactory job of giving me pain relief for months now, and although the steroids and corresponding endorphins were keeping my addictive mind active and content, my addiction history had always been that I'd soon get bored with being in the same mental plateau for any sustained period of time and, like Columbus, feel a need to explore something more exciting.

It had been literally twenty years since sending the Iceman packing after the brutal weekend binge when David was a year old. So, trying to fathom why I'd want to return to Sheol, even possibly entertain the thought of inviting the demon back now that I was finally seeing some light, defies all human logic.

I was alone, I was bored, and I was also experiencing some lower back pain that the pump wasn't able to solve (most likely an addict illusion). Also, the excitement of the new physical fitness lifestyle and the steroid high had worn off. So what to do? I called my weed connection and asked him if he knew anyone who could get me some cocaine. I explained that my back pain had returned, and I was just looking to get some temporary quick relief. Just as I had suspected, he came through with the name and phone number of an old acquaintance of mine, who, like me, had also been an addict himself pretty much all his life. I anxiously called him, promptly got re-acquainted, explained my situation, then popped the big question.

As had been the norm all of my adult life, the devil read my mind and, having waited a season, directed me straight to my fix like a shark to blood. Within an hour, I was in a bathroom stall at Josh and Molly's restaurant/bar (Burlington, New Jersey) snorting cocaine. That very first line hit me like an arrow to the liver! All the old nightmarish memories came flooding back instantly, beginning with the nasty bitter cocaine drip taste in the back of the throat that all coke freaks come to know and love.

Two decades earlier, God had showed me His enduring mercy by allowing me to live through way too many cocaine binges than I care to remember. So, how did I express my gratitude to Him for keeping my family together after all the coke coaster rides of yesteryears? I didn't. It was almost like all those crazy nights fearlessly running the streets in search of my next nosebleed had never really happened, as if that was another life or something. Maybe it was, but again, Jesus said in Matthew 12:43–45:

> When an unclean spirit leaves a man he goes to find rest somewhere then returns to the place from which he came and when he sees that place has been cleaned up he goes and returns again with seven worse spirits even more wicked than itself and dwell there making the state of that man even worse than before.

Let's just say that during the proceeding twenty years of abstinence from the worst of my many demons, the Iceman had been doing push-ups while anxiously anticipating the return of his best customer and greatest soldier, and just as Jesus said, he surely did bring seven worse demons with him this time.

The Dealers Were My Friends . . . or Were They?

My trips to meet the dope man became as regular as a bowel movement. I suppose I felt some sort of self-control by only getting enough stuff to blast my brains out one day at a time. The problem with that philosophy is that it meant more covert missions and more chances of getting caught. The coke man was truly a very professional and reliable dealer.

Come to think of it, during all my years of confiscating illegal drugs, my dealers were all as dependable as the sun coming up in the morning. They were almost like brothers to me in some sick sorta way. I'd call him, and he always answered and was always ready to make a quick buck. He would often bless me by visiting my apartment complex to spare me a trip. He'd call when he was pulling in, and I'd coolly take Teddy for a walk just at the perfect time. He'd pull into the designated parking spot, and I'd walk over to do the old, "Hey, what's up, brother! How you been?" routine as we exchanged money and supply in one slick "dealer-doper" handshake.

If he didn't happen to be in the Mount Holly/Lumberton area, it was never a problem to have his cousin meet me at a McDonald's parking lot or one of our other routine spots (Wawa, West Coast Video, Burger King, Prospectors Restaurant) on Route 38 in Mount Laurel, all merely ten to twenty-minute round trips to paradise. I'd tell him when I was leaving and call him again a minute or so before my arrival at the agreed spot.

We used really tricky spy-like codes for the exchanges to throw off any cops listening in on our phone lines somehow; you know, really ingenious stuff like, "Hey bro, you got eight more oranges? Meet me at that spot," the code to bring me an "eight-ball" (3.5 grams) to whatever was the last drop-off spot. He knew my car, so he was always lurking somewhere in the vicinity, scoping things out, then when he and I both felt undetected, I'd park in an unsuspicious spot, then he'd pull into the lot and park right next to me as I sat anxiously in my car. He'd then get out and hop into my car for the exchange. I would often cruise through the drive-in to get food prior to parking to camouflage the real purpose of my existence there.

Oh, the paranoia of the drug world . . . what a thing of beauty! We were a well-oiled machine. We made exchange after exchange, pretty much on a daily or every other day basis, without ever even coming close to getting caught. The idea of a felony drug possession charge never really occurred to me. I had never been arrested except for the DUI when I was in my mid-twenties after overindulging at an open bar company Christmas party and driving home on the wrong side of the highway, narrowly missing a head-on collision with a Corvette.

I honestly didn't even know what the consequences of a felony arrest warranted and never really contemplated the seriousness of my behavior. I would find out in the very near future what the seriousness of it was, however.

The Horrors of Addiction

While in the midst of a major coke binge, there was an incident that particularly frightened me. It occurred as I sat in the living room of my apartment, snorting line after line in a manner that would have put Ray Liotta in *Good Fellas* to shame.

I was going at it pretty much nonstop, line after line, as was my normal routine, until I prepared to take another "boot," and while inserting the approximately four-inch large straw into my left nostril, I noticed it wouldn't stop. It kept sliding and sliding farther up into my head until the entire straw disappeared.

What in the world was going on? How was I going to get it out? Was I having another hallucination? I was freaking out! It was no hallucination. The entire straw had slid up into my head. The constant cocaine snorting had blown a hole clear through to my sinuses. I was so high that I thought maybe I was just imagining it. So, I paused for a minute, then after fetching the disappearing straw with a pair of tweezers, I slowly reinserted the straw again, and again, it slid all the way up into my head.

I needed to take a timeout for sure, so I got up and went into the kitchen to get a beer out of the fridge. As I bent over, reaching for it, I could feel something wet dripping on my arm. I thought maybe I had left the freezer door open, and it was condensation dripping down or something. That was until I looked down and saw blood splattering on the kitchen floor between my legs and all over my new Air Force Ones. What the heck was going on? It finally hit me. The blood was pouring out of my nose like a faucet had been turned on.

Oh my God! What is happening? Am I going to die? I grabbed a towel and pinched my nose closed with one hand, hoping to stop the bleeding. I then proceeded to the bathroom to wash off my sneakers with my free hand before they'd be permanently ruined, God forbid! Next, I went back to the kitchen, grabbed some ice cubes, put them in the towel, and headed to the couch to lay down with my head tilted back, hoping I wouldn't die but not really caring if I did.

I lay there absolutely astonished at what had just happened. What the heck was I going to do now? I still had a pile of blow talking to me from my coffee table, but I didn't dare try to lean over and attempt snorting it. However, maybe a line would help cauterize my nostril and stop the bleeding, I insanely reasoned. No, I couldn't risk taking the direct pressure off my nose, so I remained on my back and devised the perfect solution to my dilemma. With my head tilted back while pressing the ice bag against the left side of my nose with my left hand, I reached over and grabbed a rock of cocaine with my right hand. I then stuffed it down my right nostril and vehemently inhaled it down my throat. Bingo! Problem solved. That was the system of delivery I used for the rest of the night until the pile had vanished and I passed out. Wow! I had taken the term "addict" to a level of extreme that was incomprehensible, even to myself.

The kids were going to be visiting in a couple of days, and here I was with a scab running from my left nostril to my lip. It looked like someone had taken a blow torch to me. How would I explain that? No problem; the liar would handle it. I had been complaining about my sinus problems for months, and the kids had the pleasure of witnessing many of my other minor nose bleeds, so the stage was set.

I called my wife and explained the horror of the previous night. I told her that while blowing my nose, I developed a severe nose bleed that wouldn't stop, so I was forced to go to the emergency room in the middle of the night to have it cauterized. This explained why I sounded so exhausted on the phone and would also have the kids prepared for the visual prior to their arrival. My storytelling was possibly becoming even scarier than the truth at times, and that really was scary.

D.J. Arrived

By the time David had arrived in New Jersey for the summer, I was well on my way, ripping and racing again. I wasn't drinking and was only smoking weed occasionally and taking antidepressants and sleeping pills, but my cocaine habit was progressing steadily.

The first few weeks with him were wonderful! We would often go to breakfast at a diner nearby to get reacquainted again, reminisce, and bond as father and son. I also got him a membership at my gym, and we went nearly every morning to work out together, something that we had never done before. By then, I was pretty well pumped up on the juice and was proudly showing off for my oldest son by out lifting most of the younger Hulk wannabees. He was impressed to see his father was well on his way to recovery. I remember him telling me later that he "was loving it!" I was loving it probably even more.

His girlfriend Krystalo was still attending nearby Burlington Township High School, where they had originally met. He would always pick her up after school and spend the rest of the day with her or his other high school friends.

This was a perfect scenario for me. I could spend quality time with him each morning, then I was free to spend un-quality time alone with the Iceman the rest of the day until he returned in the late evening.

Then it happened. The cocaine took complete control of me again, only this time, it was much worse than the first go-around twenty years earlier. I began going on binges where I would go days without food or sleep. The money I was receiving from unemployment had run out long ago, so I was now dipping into my retirement money to pay my expenses, and I was dipping into it like it was a bottomless pit. The couple of toothpick-sized lines of cocaine that I had snorted in Josh and Molly's to jumpstart my worst enemy had now metamorphosized into regular $300 eight-balls almost daily.

I always received pure cocaine rock (no additives or "cut") from my supplier by means of threatening to buy elsewhere, and he never disappointed.

During one of the many *Candid Camera* moments while David was living with me, I overdosed on a combination of Ativan, Ambien, and coke, and while in the bathroom, I passed out and fell and put my head through the bathroom wall. When I came to, I staggered to the living room couch and again passed out.

The next morning when David went to use the bathroom, he asked, "What happened to the wall, Dad?" I honestly didn't remember and had no answer for him, but the dried blood on my forehead was a dead giveaway.

I began to wear sunglasses to the gym to hide my sleepless eyes. When D.J. inquired, "Why the sunglasses?" I informed him, "Cause it's cool!" It was like I was trying to start a new fashion trend or something.

I specifically remember trying to get up on a Monday morning for our scheduled workout but just not having the strength. I had spent the entire weekend devouring only the drug, and its toll was becoming devastating.

I informed David as he was getting ready to leave for the gym, "I gotta sit this one out, son. My sinuses are killing me. I'll go tomorrow, though. I promise." I could feel his disappoint as he left the apartment alone that morning. Unfortunately, that was only the beginning. The next day, as he pleaded with me again to go to the gym, I snapped at him, "Cut me a break! I'm still not feeling well! I'll go tomorrow!"

He cried out, "Dad, you've been saying that for two weeks!" I argued that it had only been a couple days, and he, again, desperately trying to motivate me, repeated, "It's been weeks, Dad!"

I didn't know how to respond. It was one of my scariest moments in a long line of scary moments as an addict. I had lost two weeks and could not remember a thing.

I never again, even to this day, went to a gym to work out with my son David.

Adam Arrived

For weeks prior to Adam's arrival, I was filled with such excitement and anticipation. I had been prepared for David's initial college departure but didn't expect the lengthy separation from Adam. It was extremely hard on us both in every way, and I desperately wanted to mend the wounds I had caused him.

However, by the time the day had finally come, my emotions had completely shut down. I had no feelings whatsoever, not just toward Adam but toward anyone or anything. I just wanted to be alone with my demons. All of my thoughts and intentions were directed at only two things: getting the drug and using it.

The hallucinations became scarier and more frequent as I spent day after day without sleep, but I couldn't stop the wicked cycle I had started.

Each night, I would constantly text my sons to confirm their whereabouts to avoid being caught in the act by them. I often would coerce them into sleeping over at their friends' houses in an effort to share my apartment alone with Teddy and my demons.

Paranoia

The paranoia that a severe cocaine addict experiences can be terri-fying, to say the least. I remember one night seeing a face staring at me from the gold door knob on the front door of my apartment. As I stared back at it, I began talking to it to let it know that its cover was blown. It also must have noticed that I noticed it because it was talking right back to me. It continued staring right at me, and I was mesmer-ized as I tried to understand what it was saying since I couldn't hear its words. I would turn my head away, hoping that it would go away or possibly to trick it into believing I hadn't noticed it. Possibly, the authorities, or maybe the neighbors, I reasoned, had caught on to my peculiar habit of staying up all night and frequently, sometimes non-stop, peaking suspiciously through my window shades. I would alter-nate from the front door peephole to the living room window to the kitchen to the bathroom and then to the bedroom.

Around and around, I would go all night long as I sweated profusely with the fear of being caught. After gazing back and forth at the face for several minutes, I finally got up to take a closer look and see if I could possibly hear what it was saying. I walked right up to the door and knelt down to stare at the face, face-to-face. It was only then that I realized that I truly was under surveillance. The face I had been staring at, the face that had been spying on me for most of the night, was my own. Just as it had been since first entertaining that big blue bong in 1979, the only thing I ever had to fear was myself.

Another night, as I peered out the blinds of my living room, I saw a *Close Encounters of the Third Kind*-type spaceship land in the court-yard of our complex. It was all lit up with all the colors of the rainbow and blinking and flashing, reminiscent of a Metallica concert. It was only when aliens began descending out of the ship's hatch that I closed the blinds and hid for cover. I'm thankful that the kids weren't around to witness my insanity, well, at least not always, they weren't.

One night, as I peered through my front door peephole, I observed a police officer with a big DEA-type dog approach my door. I had suspected for months that they had had me under surveillance ever since the drinking episode several months earlier and somehow had picked up on my extremely peculiar behavior.

I quickly ran into the bedroom in the middle of the night to awaken David and confessed that the police were at my door. When he irritably questioned, "Why would the police be at your door, Dad?" I could only nervously respond, "I don't know!"

He promptly jumped out of bed, went directly to the front door, opened it, then turned to me and despondently said, "Look, Dad, there's no one there!"

I slowly stuck my head out the door and looked to the right and the left for confirmation. What a relief . . . I had escaped prosecution once again.

I had no idea how the drug sniffers disappeared so abruptly and without a trace, but I could now stop sweating and shaking and get back to the task at hand: inhaling the remainder of my pile of blow.

Schizophrenia

Dr. Buck had diagnosed me with several conditions during the time that he was my primary physician based solely on lab tests and the disinformation I was feeding him. However, to my shame, I never admitted to him my addiction issues and its accompanied side effects. I hid from him, and everyone who knew me, the one disease that was the scariest, the most severe of them all, paranoid schizophrenia.

Paranoia not only had me talking to doorknobs and running from aliens and imaginary narcotic detection canines, but it also filled me with suicidal urges and made me terrified to even open the window shades in the morning. Darkness was my canopy, and the light petrified me.

Darkness does not like the light of any kind. The Bible says, "For everyone who does evil hates the light for fear that his deeds will be exposed" (John 3:20). That Scripture described me to the tee. I certainly hated the light and feared that anyone, including Dr. Buck, might notice the evil realm I was living in.

Even if I had admitted to Dr. Buck my deepest, darkest secrets, I doubt there was much he could have done except for Baker Acting me to the nearest nut house. He was already pumping me full of psychiatric meds for my various illnesses, and just like any other drug I was using, I abused them all to the max.

No Child Should Have to See What Mine Did

I honestly never knew my children had any awareness of my partying obsession, before or after the separation, even though they often reminded me that my nose was bleeding. They even took an ominous picture of me once, passed out on the couch at my apartment with blood running down my lip, and texted it to their mother.

Maybe it was their way of trying to reach out to me? They acted as if it was funny, although I doubt their mom could find the humor in it, having borne witness to this type of behavior for nearly three decades.

I don't know if they ever really grasped the acrimony of my problem; however, neither of my children were born stupid, and even so, they would have had to have been born blind, deaf, and dumb not to know that I had been mixing pills, booze, and marijuana for several years. However, the more erratic my behavior became, the more suspicious they had become of an even more serious problem.

I Dropped the Ball Again

During my sons' summer stay with me, David especially was beginning to watch my every move. At bedtime, he would keep the bedroom door cracked open despite my attempts to keep it shut so I could party all night in peace. Throughout the night, I'd catch him peeping around the corner of the doorway into my living room in an effort to catch me in the act. I was a very keen addict, though, and would close my eyes when hearing him tip-toeing toward the doorway, then would wait for the sound of him climbing back into bed before proceeding with my party. This routine would go on all night sometimes.

Then one morning as I lay on the couch pretending to be sleeping, although having only shut my eyes briefly the entire night due to the hide-and-seek episodes with D.J., he came into the living room to talk with me, no, plead with me would be a better description. He could barely hold his head up from exhaustion. His eyes were red and swollen from a night of obvious crying and distress.

He started by calmly saying, "Dad, you're a coke addict." I was so taken back that I couldn't even answer him. I just bowed my head in shame. I then tried to defend my behavior.

"I only take the drugs the doctors prescribe me. I know they make me a little messed up sometimes, but I'm fine," I said.

He then really broke down. "Don't you think I worry every single day that I'm gonna come home and find my dad dead? Do you ever think about that?"

No, to be honest, it had never crossed my selfish mind.

He didn't appreciate my lying very much and disgustedly told me, "I looked on the internet, and you have all the symptoms of a coke addict, Dad!" He was now crying and continued, "I don't want you to end up like Eric's dad!" His friend Eric's dad had died that past year after a long bout with cocaine addiction.

"Do you wanna get help, Dad? I know where you can get help!"

I really did want help. I truly did want to get out of the living hell I was in, if not for myself, for my sons. So I sat there on the couch silent for a moment, contemplating my answer while shaking my head back and forth in disgust at myself and at the obvious pain I was causing my son.

Finally, I answered him, "Yea, I wanna get help, son."

He said, "Do you wanna go now? We can go right now! There's a place downtown where Eric's dad used to go. I can take you."

I agreed, and we both quietly got dressed as to not awaken Adam, who was still sleeping in the bedroom. We then got into my car, and he drove me to a drug counseling facility on Main Street in Mount Holly. For the first time in over twenty-eight years of addiction, I took a sincere step toward getting real help, and it was only because of the outpouring of love from my oldest son.

He parked the car in front of the facility, and as we both walked toward the front door, I actually felt relief that I was finally going to do what was necessary to get well. I was so weak from the lack of sleep that David practically had to hold me up as we approached the door.

When we finally reached it, we were in utter amazement to learn that they were closed that day. Neither of us could believe it, but it was surely more discouraging for him than me. I can't describe the look of deflation he wore. He was leaving the following day to return to Florida for school and must have felt like this may have been his last opportunity to save his dad's ship, which was uncontrollably sinking.

We climbed back into the car and drove back to my apartment. Not one word was said between us during the ten-minute ride. When we got there and he parked, I waited for him to turn the car off before assuring him, "I won't drop the ball on this, son. I promise."

Oh, the craziness of addiction! The fear of facing this world combined with the fear of leaving it behind; the constant desire to stop the insanity, but at the same time being powerless to exercise the free will to "just say no." That's all it ever was, and is, a choice, yet it never felt like one.

I had a deeply embedded desire to see how far out on the edge I could go yet also a horrifying fear of falling. There was always an inner fear of myself, I suppose, yet it was combined with an exhilaratingly powerful excitement of pushing the limits all at the same time, not wanting to live but not wanting to die either—a state of purgatory, I suppose, the perfectly complete oxymoron.

Is it really fear that drives an addict into oblivion, or is it simply a morbid desire for pleasure? I mean, why do some women possess one hundred pairs of shoes yet continue shopping for them at every opportunity? Or why does someone visit Disney World every single year even though the park hasn't changed since the day it opened fifty years ago and they have already been to Cinderella's Castle a gazillion times? Why does someone who is one hundred pounds overweight order the supersized double quarter pounder meal with a Diet Coke? Doesn't everyone have their own idiosyncrasies that they know aren't good for them but persist on doing them anyway? Even Apostle Paul confessed, "The good I will to do I don't do, but the evil I hate, that I do" (Rom. 7:19), and he was an apostle, for goodness' sake. What makes an addict any different from anyone else? Well, I suppose another pair of shoes won't stop your heart, although another supersized #5 meal and Space Mountain just might.

The following day, Krystalo drove D. J. back to the airport, and as was the norm for me, I quickly reneged on my promise.

As is the case with any binge addict, I believe, who uses and overdoses, a day or so after having passed the chance of finality, you get a full day's sleep, your head clears, and you experience a feeling of relief and hope. It's almost another sort of high . . . a false high. You quickly begin feeling good again physically, possibly by the absence of the demons, and mentally forget the nightmare of your previous binge, almost as if it never happened.

You drop your guard again and quickly allow the "dark voice" to draw you supernaturally back into believing that one more last binge won't hurt anything . . . one more, and that will be it. You grab your sobbing and crying mask and put on a performance that Sir Lawrence Olivier would be jealous of. You vehemently swear to your loved ones that you'll never put them through that again.

"That's it! That's the last time!" I convinced myself of that lie over and over again for twenty-eight years. I had performed and refined the routine so many times over the years that it nearly always had my wife convinced, I thought. When the reality is that we both were merely filled with false hope.

Not Exactly a Honeymoon

While the kids were visiting me in Jersey (about halfway through their stay), I planned a trip down to Florida to be alone with my wife for a week. We were both excited about the trip. It would be the first time that we were truly alone for that amount of time in many years, and I'm sure that she viewed it as an opportunity to spend a lot of quality time together to work on our problems. I, on the other hand, had only one objective for the trip . . . sex.

I picked up an eight-ball for the flight, which I hid comfortably in my crotch prior to boarding. I was pretty high and feeling invisible as I strolled fearlessly undetected through the security inspections and onto the plane to take my seat. To be honest, getting busted never entered my mind. I just wanted to enjoy the ride down without jeopardizing my buzz and succeeded beyond expectation. I made it to my seat smoothly, and so as not to draw any unwanted attention, sat there patiently for the flight to take off.

After the wheels were up and we were on our way, I began making periodic trips to the boys' room to further entice the trip. I have no idea how many trips I made, but by the time we hit Tampa International, I was well lit and all out of blow. As usual, once I started snorting, I could never stop or save even a little bit for later.

My wife picked me up, and I don't even remember if we went out to dinner or not. I had my mind set on a honeymoon night, as had become the norm during this phase of our marriage, but especially now during a cocaine binge, my nucleus accumbens (part of the brain that gives sexual arousal) were at a peak, and I just wanted to get naked. When we got to her place and got settled in, we lay on the couch to watch some TV, and as usual, my evil twin took over.

My hands almost immediately went where no hands of a gentleman have any business going. She tried not to ruin the moment but quickly became uncomfortable with my groping and squirmed uncomfortably. She kept moving my hands to more appropriate places, then sensing my motives, calmly asked, "Can't we just watch TV together?" It was a reasonable request to most people, especially since she had worked all day and had to be at work again in the morning. However, a coke addict doesn't accept reason very well, especially when they have been focusing on an evening of fantasy for over 1000 miles and for many days.

Finally frustrated at having all of my sexual advances thwarted, I exploded. I was throwing "f-bombs" faster than any fastball I had ever thrown during my prime. Mr. Hyde had shown up in full force, and he was in no mood for rejection. I practically threw her out of my way and stomped my way down the hall to D.J.'s bedroom and slammed the door shut! I was done for the night, and so were we. You see, my anger really had nothing to do with her rejection. I was already beginning to "Jones" (withdraw) for more of the drug, and knowing that I was going to have to wait a whole week for my next fix, I wanted to touch the pinnacle of the high that night with the culmination of sex.

I didn't sleep much that night. Everything was going one hundred miles an hour within my sick mind.

In the morning, as soon as she had left for work, I called the airline to reschedule my flight. I had to get outta there as quickly as possible. I was Jonesing bad by now, and as drug addicts typically do, I had found an out to get back home for more dope.

It was all her fault, as usual. All she had to do was pacify me with a one-night stand, and all would have been well. But no, she had to reject her pig of a husband and would now have to face his wrath.

I had found a flight out that afternoon and even quickly located a taxi service to shuttle me back to the airport so that my ashamed alter ego wouldn't have to face my wife and risk her talking me out of my plan of exile.

I called her cell and left an angry message, detailing, "I've had it! I'm heading home!" She quickly called me back, but I wouldn't answer. "I'd fix her," I told myself.

I can still hear the message she left me. "Don't go, Dave. Please don't go! I thought we would spend a nice week together, just the two of us."

For so many years, I wanted to know for sure that she still loved me, and although she had proved it time and time again, I was never fully convinced. Here I finally had her begging me for sympathy, yet it wasn't enough. Maybe my frustration never had anything to do with my wife's love for me. Maybe it had everything to do with my lack of love for myself. I hated what I had become and had convinced myself that she hated me as well.

I called D.J. to inform him of how rudely his mom had treated me (it was always her fault) and that I had decided to come back home. He may have been even more disappointed than my wife was when I told him to be ready to pick me up at the Philly airport that evening.

He also pleaded with me to stay. "Don't do that, Dad! Give it a couple of days! You just got there," he said. Then, as if reading my mind, added, "Don't think you're coming back here to do more drugs! You'll never see Adam if you do! I can't let him see that." Wow! My oldest son, at nineteen years of age, was already more of a man and more responsible than his old man.

"Just be ready to pick me up tonight," I ordered him. I changed the flight, called the cab, then called and told my wife. She answered this time and, when informed again of my plans, sadly said, "I can't believe you're doing this." I left her and most likely whatever had been left of our shattered marriage in Tampa Florida that day.

My Return Home

When I got back to New Jersey, I picked up right where I had left off. The kids were only there a couple more weeks, and I barely saw them anyway. Oh, we had a token dinner get-together occasionally at Friday's in Mount Holly or Houlihan's in Cherry Hill, but I was way lost. I was constantly high on cocaine and rarely slept. Even when I'd drive to meet them somewhere, I'd always snort some junk in my car before going in and then would also make several trips to the men's room to keep my high up. I would always practically gag my food down from a lack of appetite. When I was in the middle of a "snow ride," I could barely do or focus on anything else but the drug. It was my sustenance.

I Wanted My Family Back

It was the end of August 2006 when I finally had had enough of being a long-distance husband and father. I was watching one of Adam's Seahawks football practices (a Pop Warner league for eighth and ninth graders), and my heart was aching to be his father again and not just some guy who visited every now and then as if he was a successful traveling businessman or something.

The only traveling I was doing was in circles within my polluted mind. I had to get things back together. I had to fix what I had broken so severely. But how? My spirit had been out of sync for so long. I wasn't sure if it was even remotely possible for me to begin living a normal respectful life at the age of forty-six, and that revelation frightened me terribly.

I had gotten back into my wife's good graces (sort of) and popped the big question during another visit to Florida. "Would it be okay if I moved down?" She hesitated for a moment, which didn't give me the fuzziest feeling inside, then said, "I guess. But why now? Why'd it take you a year?"

I thought that was an interesting question since she was the one who took out the year lease for my apartment without ever consulting me. I had assumed that was my sentence for being so naughty for so long, you know, a year's restriction, a long time-out.

I responded by telling her I wasn't sure if she wanted me around since she was the one who left me to move 1000 miles away.

She countered, "You can move down," but before I had the chance to leap for joy, she drew the line in the sand, "But you can't move in with us. You've got to get your own place. That's a compromise."

I wasn't thrilled with the compromise thing, but at least she didn't object to my moving down, which gave me a glimmer of hope once again.

As soon as I returned to Jersey, I hit the internet to find housing. I had decided to investigate the USF vicinity. It was far enough away from Harbour Island (my wife's place) that she wouldn't feel threatened or pressured, and I wouldn't have to worry about her popping in to check up on my behavior.

I was also excited about the prospect of spending time with D.J. while he was on campus. After very little research, I spotted a nice complex in North Tampa on 50th Street called Park Avenue Apartments and quickly put the required deposit down.

My scheduled move-in window was early October, which gave me time to pack up my stuff and get the movers scheduled. It also gave me a little bit of time to finish my bachelorhood with a flurry before attempting to get my head right. I was finally going to buckle down, stop using, end the insanity, and restore my family.

I had it all planned out, I believed. Now, all I had to do was move down and very patiently win my family back. I was filled with fear, however. Mount Holly had been my entire life, and addiction had been the ruler of the majority of that life. Except for the one-month detox after college, I had practically zero experience with sobriety during my adulthood. This was an awful lot for a person with absolutely no willpower to handle. However, whatever decency that remained in me, as little as it may have been, was reaching into my soul and yanking me toward the south.

I had to do this. I had to at least try for once to do the right thing, the responsible thing, and attempt to live like a responsible adult. This was not going to be easy for a severely obsessive compulsive addict whose mind was lagging many years behind on the maturity scale.

Preparing to Move to Florida

A few days before the moving truck was to arrive to empty my apartment for the move, I had another out-of-this-world experience. While marijuana had unleashed the munchie demon many years prior, cocaine had always set free the sugar demon within me.

For whatever reason, cocaine always made me crave sugar. I had zero appetite for pretty much any other food that contained any nutritional value while in the midst of a coke binge, yet I had no problem inhaling any and all sugar products. Cookies, cakes, candy, milkshakes, you name it, I couldn't get enough of it. Possibly, it had something to do with the fact that I wasn't drinking and the cocaine was a trigger for alcohol, which contains sugar. I don't really know, but I do know that in recent weeks, donuts had become my sugar of choice.

It was not unusual for me to drive to the Dunkin Donuts store a mile or so down Route 38 to pick up a dozen choice meanies. I'd consume a toasted coconut and a frosted blueberry or two on the way back to my apartment. Then, in the corresponding frenzy, I'd polish off nearly all of the remaining dozen in one sitting.

It was late one night, and I was numb from head to toe when the sugar demon called me. Being defenseless against his attacks, I immediately sought to obey. It was after midnight, but I could see visions of coffee cake muffins dancing in my head, so I called Dunkin Donuts to check their availability, and sure enough, they were still open. I trust that I wasn't the only Lumberton resident who came under attack by the late-night munchie and sugar demons.

I happily grabbed my keys and swaggered, or staggered, to my car half-blind. I quickly backed out, hit the gas, and before you could say k-turn, bam! "What the heck was that!" I slammed my car shift into park mode and got out to find that I had run straight into the rear of a pickup truck that had been protruding just a bit too far out of its parking spot. It surprised the heck out of me! I never even saw it! I examined the truck and saw very minimal damage; however, the front right quarter panel, including the headlight of my car, had been knocked way out of kilter.

I sheepishly looked around, and seeing no eyewitnesses, I couldn't allow my quest to be deterred, so I quickly slid back into my car and completed the round trip to Dunkin Donuts as if nothing had ever happened.

As I sat in my apartment gorging on donuts and cocaine, there was a knock on my door. Suspecting that it was my pain-in-the-rear upstairs neighbor needing some peanut butter or something, I didn't hesitate to answer it. I covered my coke with the daily newspaper, got up, opened the door, and to my utter surprise, there stood two police officers. It was the same two officers who busted into my apartment the previous fall during the drunken binge that nearly killed me.

One of them asked me if it was my Altima parked outside. Being high as a kite but also sharp as a tack from the cocaine and knowing his question before he asked, the "liar" came instantly to my defense. I quickly confessed, "Yea, I know. I just hit a truck in the parking lot, and I wasn't sure whose it was, so I was gonna tell someone in the morning."

These two officers were true champs. Knowing my history, they asked if I had been drinking again. I proudly assured them that I hadn't drank since they rescued me during their previous visit. Then one of them asked what was wrong with my nose, as he noticed blood beginning to trickle down my lip. I wiped my nose, and without even an instant of hesitation, the "liar" responded, "Oh, I had sinus surgery today to remove some polyps." Wow! How he pulled that one out of the bag, I'll never know, but it worked.

The officers briefly looked about my apartment, and when seeing all the cardboard boxes, I explained I was moving in a couple of days.

They were satisfied, then advised me that they could have arrested me for hit-and-run, which carried some serious charges, but remembering the cupcakes my mom had made for them for saving her son, they would let me go with a careless driving ticket. Way to go, Mom! And thank goodness for the *Burlington County Times* that had concealed at least a couple more felony charges that would have consummated a really banner evening.

It was a day or so later when the movers came and emptied my apartment of all of my belongings to deliver to my new apartment in Tampa. The plan was that we would meet down there in a couple of days. They had other stops, so we promised to stay in contact with each other along the way to navigate the move smoothly.

I spent the last night in my apartment sleeping on the floor with Teddy, a pillow, and a blanket. I didn't sleep very well that night, to say the least.

I was filled with anxiety in anticipation of starting my new life away from the only town that I had ever called home. It was going to be a completely new life, free from drugs and alcohol for the first time in twenty-eight years. I am not sure which of these two revelations scared me the most, but I was determined to get my precious family back, and the move south appeared to be the only option I had left. The power of darkness, however, remained very real and very powerful upon me.

When I awoke in the morning, I was shaking with cold sweats. I was paralyzed on the floor as if the blanket I had covering me was made of lead. I absolutely could not get off the floor. It had me frozen there, shaking.

My wife called me mid-morning and asked, "Are you on your way yet?"

I can only imagine what she must have thought when I responded in terror, "I can't move! I can't get off the floor!" I literally felt as if something beyond myself was pinning me to the floor, and I was powerless against my opponent. She must have been so confused but merely requested that I give her a call when I was on the way. I would only learn a day or so later the true motive of her call and questioning.

I kept telling myself, "I've got to get up! I've got to get moving!" I had no choice at this point. Everything I owned was on its way to Florida, so I couldn't procrastinate much longer, or it would jeopardize the coordination of my move and delay the ignition of my game plan to regain the life I had lost, a life with my family.

When I told Teddy that we had to get going, he jumped up and cutely began dancing in circles as he often did, knowing it meant he'd have the opportunity to go outside.

Such a small privilege to him, you would think, but the preceding months had relegated him to a life mostly in a dark, curtain-drawn apartment, watching his master live in a prison within himself. Teddy always did have more strength than me, and it was only his excitement that finally allowed me to pry myself free from that apartment floor.

I quickly jumped up, grabbed the rest of my things, and it was my hope, as I left that apartment, that I had locked the door behind me to the demons that had bound me for nearly three decades.

I had gotten as far as Georgia when I decided to stop at a tiny roadside motel for the night. I called my wife to advise her of my progress, and she burst out crying. I asked her what was wrong, and she could barely voice the words, "I filed for divorce today."

Acting like I didn't hear her, or maybe it was that I didn't want to hear her, I tried to console her, "Please don't cry, sweetheart." I asked, "What? What's wrong?"

While continuing to cry, she said, "I came all the way down here to get away from you, and now you're here! You said to give you until September to get saved, and I gave you even longer, and you haven't changed."

I was scared to death! For a decade or so, our marriage had struggled as we drifted further and further apart, but I never seriously considered we'd ever get divorced. We were soulmates. We were meant for each other. Even as she uttered the words, in my heart, I believed she'd change her mind, and we'd work things out as we always had. Maybe I was just so terribly confused about us. Maybe only I still considered us to be a special pair. Maybe I was the only one who had been in love all those years. Was this really happening? Was my wife of twenty-four years really going to divorce me?

Welcome to the Sunshine State

On October 15, 2006, I arrived at the Park Avenue apartments. D.J. had warned me early on that it wasn't the best of neighborhoods, especially compared to their residence within the exclusive gated community of Island Walk on Harbour Island. I suppose pretty much any neighborhood would seem like the hood in comparison. Although Park Avenue was a big step up from the Whitehall development I had just left, it was light-years away from the 5000-square-foot property in Oxmead Crossing where my family was last united.

The movers arrived at nearly the same time, and the move went exceptionally smooth. The complex was right across the street from the University of South Florida campus that David attended, which had been the major consideration why I had chosen it. I was hoping I'd be spending a lot of time with him. I still wasn't working as I waited for the outcome of my Social Security disability case to pop. I had plenty of free time on my hands and was certainly expecting to spend much of it with him while he was on campus. Yet, I apparently had burnt down any remaining bridges between me and my firstborn, and during my tenure at Park Avenue, I was never visited by David or anyone else from my family.

Meeting Willie

A day or so after my arrival, a neighbor downstairs named Willie greeted me. It's absolutely scary at times how when you're living in darkness that it will follow you wherever you go. Trust me, the devil is very real.

Willie knocked on my door to introduce himself. He was carrying a small box, and upon opening it to entice my eyes, he pointed to the marijuana and other various goodies that it contained and asked, "Do you need any candy?" I was shocked! He didn't even know me. I could have been a cop. I was surprised at his boldness, but maybe he did know me after all. Maybe I had that look, the look of a twenty-eight-year addict. Either way, I couldn't fall so quickly, so easily, so I responded, "I'm good, man. I quit all that stuff. Thanks anyway, though." He let me know that if I changed my mind, I could always find him downstairs.

The following day, he knocked on my door again. This time, he wanted to know if I could give him a ride. It was only about five minutes away, he said, so I agreed. He had to stop at a friend's house over on 22nd Street to "get a few things." I didn't know it at the time, but 22nd Street was a well-known drug neighborhood. We pulled up at his buddy's apartment building, and I waited in the car while he went in. When he returned to the car, I noticed he wasn't carrying anything. I knew right away that he only went to make a dope deal.

As I drove away, he immediately pulled out a short glass tube, placed something in it, and began lighting it right in front of me. I said, "What's that?" He informed me that it was "crack." I instructed him not to smoke in my car. I had never seen crack before, but I knew I sure didn't want to take any chances of getting pulled over by the police while he was sparking up a rock. It was very clear that Willie had a major habit. He couldn't get that junk in him quick enough.

When we got back to Park Avenue, he followed me upstairs to my place, and before I knew what was happening, he walked right in and began lighting it up again. I told him to "hurry up and get going!" He asked me if I wanted some, but for the second time, I denied his temptation. I had done plenty of drugs and had a love affair with cocaine, but I had heard many terrible tales about crack, how it will "drain" you, and I wasn't willing to go down that road. Besides, I was cleaning up my life and starting over fresh.

My new life was very short-lived, however. The boredom of sobriety moved into my new residence in just a matter of days, and the voice of the coke demon was still very clear within my soulless frame.

I invited Willie upstairs upon making another ill-fated choice and copped a little weed, just a little something to "hold me over," I told him.

Willie soon asked me for another ride to his friend's house, but this time, I joked that I'd have to charge him. I asked him if he could get me a one-hundred-dollar piece of crack. He was more than happy to. I suppose he could spot a sucker a mile away. He knew I had never smoked crack before, which also meant I had no idea what a one-hundred-dollar piece looked like. We took the quick ride over to 22nd Street to pick up what I learned to be the devil himself.

When we got back to my apartment, Willie loaded up his "stem" and taught me the proper technique to destroy whatever remained of my soul. I took a big hit, held it in, then exhaled. Willie was exhorting me, "Do you feel it, man?" Then he started hitting the stem as well. However, he appeared as if he was in heaven itself, while I just sat there looking at him and waiting for my own euphoria. He kept asking, "Do you feel it?"

I answered, "No, it ain't doin' nothing for me!" I was expecting the normal cocaine high that I received from snorting powder cocaine, but when the one-hundred-dollar piece was gone in an instant, so was Willie. I just sat there, thinking, "What an idiot! I just blew one hundred dollars!"

I wasn't to be denied, however. I called Willie the next day and told him I wanted to get some more, $200 this time. Again, we took the ride over to 22nd Street, did the dirty deed, and returned to my place. This time, however, I didn't invite Willie in. I had predetermined that either I was going to get high off of this stuff or that was it for the crack experiment. Either way, Willie the moocher wasn't going to hit and run my stuff this time.

I didn't have a stem, but I had been a dope addict long enough to know how to make a tin foil pipe. Apparently, the tin foil pipe was the clincher. I remember lighting the rock, and when the flame began growing, the rock began glowing, almost like a charcoal briquette does when it's ready. I then blew out the flame and sucked in a big lungful of crack smoke. Pow! I had heard about the instant rush that crack gives when it hits your bloodstream, and I had witnessed such a phenomenon while watching Willie light up, but now I truly experienced the myth. It was entirely different from snorting cocaine rock. It was a new high, a higher high, that now owned me. I was literally seeing stars!

The Hall of Fame Ceremony

It was in the spring of 2006 that I received the long anticipated letter from my alma mater. I was voted into the R.V.R.H.S. Sports Hall of Fame. I never got drafted by a Major League team and never even had the chance to play in the minor leagues, but being elected into the Hall was the biggest achievement of my athletic career. I was truly honored to be joining my brother and the other R.V. greats like Franco Harris.

The ceremony was scheduled for November 3, 2006, at Charley's Other Brothers, a popular local restaurant a few weeks after I had arrived at my new place in Tampa. It was a truly wonderful affair. All my family was there. My mom and dad, my brother and his wife, my sons, and even my wife showed me some respect by joining us.

In my induction speech, I started by thanking my dad for not allowing me to quit baseball as an eight-year-old. I thanked my mom for always cleaning my dirty uniforms. I thanked my brother for never letting me win any time we competed at anything as kids, and I praised my sons for being the wonderful children they had always been. I thanked my wife as well.

I had rented out a hotel room for my family for the weekend; however, my wife refused and took my sons to stay at her parents' house instead. God forbid we could pretend to be a real family on one of the greatest occasions of my life, so I was left all alone in the hotel room. And true to the saying, "Idle hands are the devil's workshop," the devil was again about to go to work.

I couldn't hit up my old coke connection fast enough, and just like old times, we connected effectively and efficiently behind the McDonald's like a well-oiled machine, and I spent the night after the ceremony in my room alone, snorting away. I even brought a pocketful with me on the plane to enjoy on the trip back to Florida. I once again made continuous trips to the bathroom and sniffed and snorted the entire trip back.

Adam's Concussion

On a Saturday night, nine days (11/11/06) after being inducted into the Hall of Fame, my wife and I were at one of Adam's Seahawks football games. Going to those games together felt just like old times except that after being on the sideline coaching my sons for so many years, I was now reduced to watching from the bleachers. Although Adam was a high school freshman, Plant High did not have a freshman team, so rather than sit on the bench for the JV or varsity teams, he elected to play in the fifteen-year-old and under Bay Area Pop Warner League. He had gotten discouraged the season before (his first in Florida) playing for the Hurricanes team while living in the West Chase section of Tampa and quit halfway through the season.

Now that his mother had relocated them to the Harbour Island section of town, he decided to give football another try. Again, he became discouraged as his coach had him alternating as quarterback, but by halfway through the season, he was the full-time starter and caught fire. The team ran off five straight wins to make the playoffs, and Adam was carrying them on his back with his arm, and his legs.

In the previous game, he ran for a touchdown, made a diving catch for a touchdown, ran for an extra point, passed for an extra point, and then to cap off a once-in-a-lifetime game, he drove his team down the field and completed a game-winning touchdown pass as time expired. It may very well have been the greatest game he had ever played. The win propelled his team into the playoffs, which, in itself, was a miracle, considering they started the season at 0-4.

They played the Bills on this night, and while we had been watching the game, I received numerous calls from Willie. He needed a ride over to 22nd Street again. My wife, sounding suspicious, asked me why someone was calling me so much on a Saturday night. I told her it was my pain-in-the-butt neighbor who's always begging for rides. I texted Willie that I'd get back to him after the game.

I must admit it was ironic to see my wife with a sense of jealousy about her. I was the one who always observed so intently every time her phone rang or beeped from an incoming text message. I admittedly enjoyed seeing the shoe on the other foot. Although it was most likely her intuition of my craftiness and not jealousy that had her suspicions aroused, I suppose it was the suggestion that she possibly may have cared, if she was indeed jealous, that gave me some sort of rise.

It can be scary at times how quickly and abruptly our life's course can turn from the highest highs to the lowest lows in sports and in life. The Seahawks Cinderella run was short-lived.

Adam had another great game, yet the team came up a couple of points short, and their season ended. Adam also took a couple of really hard hits on back-to-back plays while running the ball, and although he popped right back up, he was noticeably woozy.

He finished the game, but as my wife and I walked to the concession stand area to wait for him, a parent came running over to us hysterically to inform us he had collapsed on the field. Our hearts both stopped for an instant! I ran out to the field to a crowd of people who had formed a circle around him. He was awake and sitting up but said he had a bad headache. There was a physician on sight who examined him but felt he was okay enough to go home. We were instructed to merely keep an eye on him for a few hours and, if there was any change in his condition, to rush him to the ER.

Since Adam appeared to be okay, and my wife wasn't keen to the idea of me coming back to her place to help keep an eye on him, I was free to go assist in Willie's crack deal.

Adam would not play football again until his senior year at Plant High School. And although he was on a team that won the state championship that year, he was a backup wide receiver and rarely got to play. I remember my wife saying that it was our fault. The truth is it was entirely my fault. I had always coached Adam and practiced with him regularly, but after our separation, I'd never coach him again, and he lost interest in sports.

D.J. would have the opportunity to play baseball for four years in high school and was very good. Adam, however, was the best athlete I had ever coached, and his potential was unlimited.

One of my greatest regrets in a lifetime filled with regrets is the fact that he never got to fulfill that potential because of me.

First Arrest in Florida

I suppose a normal-thinking person would have merely been thankful that their precious son had survived such a scary moment and called it a night. But I was far from being able to "read the signs" and even further from being normal, so I anxiously flew back up Route 275 to get Willie. Apparently, he wasn't the only one the crack demon was talking to that fateful Saturday night only a week after my Hall of Fame induction.

I phoned him on the way to give him the heads up that I also wanted in on the party. "Put me down for a hundred-dollar piece," I boasted. I made a stop at the Bank of America ATM on Fowler in the flea market parking lot off Nebraska Avenue. I grabbed my share for the deal, then headed to get Willie.

Good ole Willie, I would learn later, was further invested in crack hell than even I had suspected. He had been arrested numerous times for crack offenses and was a poster child for penal system recidivism.

On this night, he was well-strung out and quite disoriented. He had absolutely no clue where we were going for the pickup. Rather than go to Biggy's (the dealer) apartment on 22nd Street, apparently there was a change of plans. He was going to use Dave's taxi service to go to a house off Nebraska Avenue to pick up some clothes he had left there.

Nebraska was a notoriously bad, poverty-filled neighborhood loitered with dealers and prostitutes. We stopped at a couple of different houses as Willie continued to become even more confused, only to come up empty. It was nearing midnight, and it felt like we were driving around in circles, knocking on random doors, and hoping somebody could cure his crack itch. I was getting frustrated with Willie and the whole ordeal in general.

As we were driving suspiciously in a back neighborhood trying to locate Biggy, I had a bad feeling in my spirit and suggested that we call off the chase and head home. Willie was one persistent crackhead, though, and talked me into one more stop. That's when the first strike came.

As we turned down an abnormally dark back street in a residential neighborhood, out of nowhere, a cop car appeared behind me. He immediately turned on his flashing bright lights, and I immediately pulled off to the side of the road. I retrieved my registration card from the glove compartment and got my license out of my wallet as he approached my car with his flashlight blaring.

It had been so long since I had been pulled over for anything that I forgot the protocol. I opened my car door, but before I could even take one step out, the officer ordered me, "Get back in your car!" Then, I noticed his partner approaching Willie's side of the car. The officer informed me that I was pulled over for having a taillight out, which I honestly wasn't aware of. Then, in sync, they both started questioning us about our intentions. It was as if they smelled our guilt a mile away. I told the officer as he took my IDs that we were going to Willie's friend's house to pick up his clothes, which was only partly true but true, nonetheless.

He then asked us both to get out, put our hands on top of my car, and began searching us. They spotted my hundred dollars in Willie's pocket, which set off a new barrage of questioning about the purpose of our cruising a drug-infested neighborhood so late at night with "so much money." The officer interrogating me acted as if I was insulting him by not admitting that we were there for exactly the reason he was accusing us of. I suppose the "picking up clothes" explanation didn't sit too well with Mr. Officer. I mean, what was he expecting us to say, "Yes, Mr. Officer, sir. We're here in this drug-infested neighborhood to buy drugs. Why else would we be driving around in circles at midnight on a Saturday night? Oh, that's right! To pick up my bud Willie's clothes!"

The police officer appeared determined to fill his Saturday night quota and asked if he could search my car. Not knowing my rights,

I said, "Sure." I felt I had nothing to hide, so I might as well cooperate. They thoroughly completed their search, which came up empty, wrote me a warning for the taillight, read us the riot act again, then allowed us to go.

Relieved like a drunk at a urinal, I caught a deep breath and very slowly and cautiously drove away. I informed Willie that our expedition was over. "I'm heading home, man. We're done for the night."

But as we drove down the street, he anxiously blurted out, "That's the house! Right over there! Come on, man! It'll only take a minute!"

I countered, "Are you crazy! That cop will see us!"

He said, "He's gone! Come on!"

And as I looked in the rearview mirror, it appeared he was right. I definitely didn't want to stop, but I definitely did want to get high. Quite the dilemma, I should say, but Willie didn't have to do much to convince me to pull up in front of our targeted house despite my better judgment. It was pitch black out, so I figured we'd go unseen even if the police car was still lurking about.

Willie got out and walked back behind the house to a point where I couldn't see him. I first waited patiently for Willie, then I gradually became antsy as he was taking much longer than expected. It seemed like he disappeared into the darkness forever. Then a guy came out from behind the house, and I hopped out to ask him where Willie was. He said he was coming, so I got back in the car.

Just as the circumstances were beginning to bring back memories of when a guy beat me for $500 worth of weed money back in the eighties, here came Willie carrying a duffle bag of clothes. He put the bag in the back seat, and we were on our way home. As we drove in anxious anticipation, my first question was, "Did you get it?" He proudly pulled out a small plastic baggy containing about ten rocks or so of the treasure we had been searching for what seemed like an eternity.

Now we just had to find our way home, which was not going to be any small task. We both had our crack blinders on now in anticipation of firing up and having neglected to leave a trail of breadcrumbs on our way over. I was still very new to the area, having lived in Tampa only a month, and although Willie had been there for years, he couldn't have picked a worse time to come down with a case of amnesia. Nebraska

Avenue was only about two miles from our apartment complex, but it ended up taking me three days to finally return to my apartment and the comfort of my best friend Teddy.

No sooner had we made two turns when there was another set of Tampa's finest right behind me with lights flashing. This would be strike two. This time, I did have something to hide. I quickly and frightfully quizzed Willie, "Where's the stuff?" He nervously said, "Don't worry; it's cool."

As soon as the officer got to my passenger side door, I was ready for him. I excitingly explained to him that I knew about the taillight and that we had just been pulled over ten minutes earlier right around the corner. When I handed him the warning ticket to cement my case, he went back to his car to confirm my alibi. After only a couple of minutes, the nice officer let us go with no hassle at all. Driving away and feeling like I had just been handed a "Get Out of Jail Free" card, which, ironically, I had, I exasperated to Willie, "I am going to get so freaking high when I get home!" Not so fast, Mr. Destruction.

I don't believe we even went one block before the third and final strike hit. The number three in the Bible stands for heavenly perfection. Although, nothing was feeling quite perfect or heavenly on this quagmire of an evening. Is it possible that it was going exactly as God wanted? I'm not sure if the previous hassle-free cop had tipped them off, but two police cars with lights flashing escorted my car into a well-lit corner gas station. This time, however, they didn't want to hear our alibi and certainly were not very nice. They had Willie and I get out of the car and quickly handcuffed us under the spotlight of an entire intersection of onlookers. One officer took Willie over to his car while another took me over to his.

By this time, another squad car had arrived as Willie and I stood amongst the flashing lights. The officers questioned Willie and I separately as two other officers went through every inch of my car, including the duffle bag on the back seat. The leader of the group then abruptly came over to me and said, "That's an awful lot of cocaine we found in your car!" I immediately put on my innocent bystander face and practically got on my knees to convince him that it wasn't my cocaine. He scoffed, "Oh, really. Your buddy said the same thing."

At that moment, a member of the search party came over to reveal that they also found two crack pipes in the duffle bag. He then admitted that Willie was no friend of mine after all, as he befittingly pleaded ignorance to the entire circumstance. I continued begging the officer, "Check the size of the clothes in the bag! That's not my bag!" Since Willie was literally half my size, surely they could decipher that the bag of clothes was his, and hence the pipes and cocaine as well. The officer was having no part of my story.

He said, "It's your car, so it's your crack." Besides, he said that the bag had contained bank statements and other personal documents of mine.

Apparently, one of two things must have happened. Either Willie had set me up by planting the rocks in the passenger side seat where they were found, and my documents that had been on the back seat in his bag, or the officers had. Either way, my goose was cooked. I wasn't going to get "so f---ing high" on this night after all.

There's something about being handcuffed and put into a police car that has an instantly sobering effect on a man.

Willie and I were placed in separate police cars and promptly driven to Orient Road Jail for booking. Amazingly, it hit me that I had just been pulled over more times in one hour than I had been in all of my previous forty-five years put together. To this day, there's just something about flashing police car lights. They can be a mile away, but the moment I lay eyes on them, I anxiously start sweating.

Willie and I arrived at the jail at almost exactly the same time, but mysteriously, Willie acted as if he never knew me or even weirder, as if he couldn't even look at me or hear me. I wondered what the officers had said to him to make him act like a zombie. If anything, I should have been blind and deaf to him. After all, I was the one being charged with three felonies, and I was the one who wanted to call it a night prior to allowing him to talk me into the fateful decision to stop at the dark house in the dark neighborhood.

I should have been home with Teddy, drinking away my frustrations, but instead, I was in an overly crowded booking room inhaling Hillsborough County Jail bologna sandwiches with dozens of other lost souls. The first time and only time I had ever been arrested (1987, DUI), they asked me some questions, took my picture, fingerprinted me, and called my wife to come pick me up. I wasn't going to be so fortunate this time. It was very clear that I was going to get the full "all-inclusive" criminal experience, and I was extremely scared of the prognosis.

How long could they keep me? What about Teddy? Would I be in there a month, a year, or would I receive a life sentence? I had no idea. This was uncharted territory for me. I did know that cocaine, unlike marijuana, was a felony, and to someone like me, a felony was the equivalent of a life sentence.

When they checked me in, they took all my "property" (phone, wallet, keys, etc.), so I had no way to contact anyone, not that I was in any hurry to publicize that I was about to become inmate #06075398. There did happen to be a couple of phones along the wall that provided a way for the arrestees to make collect calls to family, attorneys, bail bondsmen, and so on, whatever the need may be. Ordering Uber Eats was out of the question, however. Go figure.

Surprisingly, I didn't have to wait long for a phone, and like the DUI episode, the first person I attempted to contact was my wife. Unfortunately, I couldn't remember her house phone number, and collect calls can't be made to cell phones, which added greatly to my panic. No one in the entire free world except for Hillsborough County law enforcement and Willie knew of my predicament. I felt so completely helpless, like a mouse in a trap. Until it is taken away, freedom is a privilege we all take so terribly for granted, and since they don't hold court on Sundays, I was about to have at least two cold dark nights in a jail cell to hammer home that reality.

There was access to a Tampa phone book, so I anxiously searched for someone, anyone, to contact to bail me out. It was well after midnight when I located my wife's older brother's phone number. Her two brothers had been as close as blood brothers to me for over two decades. They knew that there was nothing I wouldn't do for them, and I felt the feeling was mutual. Both of them had experienced their share of missteps with the law and certainly understood the consequences of what went along with the party life. We had kept many sacred secrets between us over the years, and I was confident that this would be just another episode to add to our folklore.

After several attempts, I was shocked when he finally answered and accepted my call. He had just gotten home from a night of partying himself, so I quickly and desperately explained the situation and sincerely apologized for contacting him in the middle of the night. I honestly had no other alternative, I explained. I didn't have access to anyone else's phone number. He was my only resort. The bail had been set at $10,000, and although I had no idea what needed to be done, he was familiar with the routine and calmly promised to come bail me out in the morning after he got some sleep. "Don't worry about it. I know what to do," he promised. I had never spent a night in jail before, and I am not too proud to admit that I was scared to death of the prospect. But I was at my brother-in-law's mercy, and there was nothing else I could do but wait until morning for his salvation.

All of those years of living dangerously on the edge of the law had me naively believing that someone like me could never be in a situation like that. I mean, someone like me, like David Scott Gaskill, doesn't belong in jail. That's for murderers and rapists and other really bad people, right? But here I was, wearing an orange jumpsuit that said "Hillsborough County Jail" on the back.

This was all uncharted territory for me. Then, in the morning, after going without sleep, I repeatedly called my wife's brother to mercilessly check on his timetable. To say that I was terrified would be grossly understating my demeanor. I was petrified! Was I ever going to get out of there? And what about Teddy? He must have been equally shook when I didn't return home.

Breakfast, which I nearly threw up because of the combination of my nerves and its foul aroma, had come and gone. As lunch approached and my brother-in-law still wasn't answering, I could only ascertain that he was on his way to my rescue. But when it was now nearly dinner time, and I was still wearing orange, I began sensing abandonment. I tried calling him once more, and to my excitement and surprise, my collect call was accepted. My excitement was short-lived, however, as my wife was on the other end of the call and was not nearly as elated as myself. It was the first time in our twenty-six years together that I had spoken to her from a jail pay phone, and she was not happy in the least to share this "first time moment" with me. In fact, this first was probably going to be the last straw in my bid for a reconciliation.

I desperately pleaded my innocence to her. It was just a case of being in the wrong place at the wrong time, I explained, a very wrong place at a very wrong time. She didn't want any parts of my story, and as I begged her, crying out at one point, "You gotta get me out of here! I am going to die in here!" she coldly responded, "You are right where you belong! With all the other losers!"

Maybe she was right after all. Oddly enough, it was possibly the only place that could save me from myself, although it was not exactly what I had in mind when I had asked her for the opportunity to get "saved" many months ago. I was filled with fear, but unfortunately, it was going to take much more than a weekend in county jail to reform twenty-eight years of addiction.

The next day, the judge lowered my bond to $5000, which meant I only had to come up with $500 to have a bail bondsmen set me free. I certainly didn't have $500 cash in my property but was blessed to learn that bondsmen accept credit cards. I quickly filled out a form releasing my credit card from my property, which meant the agent had to come to the jail, sign out my card, run it, pay the $500, and voila, freedom! Well, someone had told me once that nothing happens quickly in Florida. Whoever made that profound statement certainly must have been referring to the Hillsborough County Sheriff's Office.

My bond was reduced the morning of 11/13/06, and I almost immediately contacted the bail bondsman, who then promptly came to grab my credit card like a stripper grabbing dollar bills off a bar. Silly me! I figured I'd be home in time to watch the 6:00 p.m. SportsCenter broadcast. Nope, not a chance. The entire day came and went, and here I was spending another evening on a steel bunk.

Finally, shortly after midnight, so that the jail would get their fill of another day's worth of taxpayers' dollars for housing inmate David Scott Gaskill, the deputy summoned me from my cell for my release. Wow! Finally! What a relief . . . I was going home. Teddy must have been busting a liver after being walled up in our apartment for three full days.

My bubble would soon burst, however. When I received back my property, my credit card was missing. Apparently, the bondsman still had it. It was the middle of the night, and I had thirty bucks to my name. My car had been impounded, so I flagged down a taxi that was waiting conveniently outside the jail. It was apparent that they also were well schooled on the after-midnight release routine.

I had to get to the bondsmen office to get my card, but on the way, I had a most important order of business to take care of. I commanded the taxi driver to head immediately to the closest McDonald's. I was absolutely starving! I can say, without hesitation, that the double quarter pounder with cheese, large fries, and large Diet Coke were the best I have ever devoured in my entire life. Now fat and happy, it was off to the bondsmen to get my card. This was the first time I had ever been bonded out of jail and had no idea that bail bonding was just like any other business. The cabby dropped me off at the front door, and guess what? They were closed! Now it was the middle of the night, and I had five bucks left and no credit card. But luck had always been on my side, and it was especially the case on this evening.

I walked to the front door, and guess what? It was open!

I went inside since I had nowhere else to go and slept on the floor inside. The next morning, the maid arrived to clean the office and, quite to her surprise, found me asleep. I explained to her that I was trying to get my credit card, and luck interceded again, or much rather grace, and rather than calling the police, she called the owner and let me talk to him, and he kindly instructed me that my card was in his top desk drawer and to help myself.

I walked to a nearby ATM and took out some cash and caught a cab home.

Delivering a
Cryptic Message

I told my wife, "When the money's gone, I'm gone." I remember the look on her face like it was yesterday, one of bewilderment and fear, and at the same time, as she questioned, "What do you mean?" I repeated, "When the money's gone, I'm gone." I was referring to my upcoming suicide. I had been planning it for months.

I had tried drinking myself to death, snorting myself to death, and popping (pills) myself to death, all to no avail. It seemed like nothing could kill Superman. So, I decided there was only one way out of here, out of the hell I'd been living in for so long. I would drive my car one hundred miles per hour down Fowler Avenue and into a telephone pole. Surely that would do the trick, right? I had blown almost all my retirement fund on drugs, booze, and fine dining, and now that my crack habit was pushing a grand a day, I would soon be family-less, jobless, hopeless, and broke. So I made the decision, "When the money's gone, I'm gone," and I meant it.

I remember driving over to my wife's house to see my sons to deliver an ominous message. D.J. answered the door, and when Adam appeared, I simply sobbed, "I love you guys." Then, with tears running down my face, I turned and headed toward the front door. Before I could leave, D.J., sensing something wasn't right, questioned me, "Dad, why are you telling us you love us and then just leaving?" I repeated again, as if I didn't hear his question, "I love you guys," then left.

I was still probably a week, maybe two away from being on the front page news, and although I hadn't revealed my plot to anyone in figurative language, I was certainly throwing around hints to the ones I loved the most, my wife and sons. Maybe I was yearning for sympathy. Maybe I just wanted someone to hug me tightly and say, "I love you! Please don't go!" Maybe I wanted someone to talk me out of my morbid plot, but how could they? No one knew the freakish thoughts and darkness that had come to fill my demonic selfish mind.

The old David who always had a smile on his face, the David who loved sacrificing his time daily to teach children how to succeed in sports and in life by working hard, being dedicated, determined, playing to win, and always striving to be the best they could be, the David whose sons wrote essays about in school, describing him as their "hero," had died long ago, and the weak, hopeless replacement was soon to be dead also.

There was no way out now. I was way too far gone. The day of doom was all I could focus on now. I had to get things lined up, so to speak, which makes no sense at all since I wasn't going to be around anymore anyway. Absolutely nothing made any sense at this point. There was no more "light" within me and no "good voice" or "best Friend" to talk sense to me or talk me out of it. Well, at least if He was there, I sure couldn't hear Him.

Biggy

I was so completely alone, a thousand miles away from Mount Holly, my parents, and my brother, and two trillion miles away from my wife, D.J., Adam, and my once "best Friend." I truly had no one I could call a friend. Now that my wife had become a complete stranger, the only ones I conversed with on a regular basis were Teddy and my dope man Biggy, as he liked to be referred to, even though he had absolutely no resemblance to Biggy Smalls and certainly was no friend.

Before my arrest, he had Willie introduce us. I suppose he was a tad paranoid who was buying his product and wanted to see directly, and since Willie was AWOL after our arrest, Biggy wanted to make sure his cash flow continued.

Good ole Biggy. He knew he could count on a habit that grew from $100 a day to $5000 a week within a period of three months, assuredly as the sun rose in the morning and would often flash me a glimpse of the shiny silver "44 Mag" he kept in his way too oversized baggy jeans just to keep my payments "straight" (on time). Little did he know that a bullet to my head would have been a welcomed favor at this point compared to the pole on Fowler and the torture that the devil and his crack pipe had been afflicting me with.

You know you're a true "dope fiend" when your dealer begins to fear you and your habit more than he enjoys taking your weekly "knot." Dope fiend probably wouldn't even begin to describe what I had become. I was going days without sleep, showering, or food. My existence, if it could be termed that, consisted of sitting in the dark with the curtains drawn, watching ESPN and the Playboy channel with a cigarette in one hand, a crack pipe in the other, and an alcoholic beverage of my choice resting comfortably within my reach. I rarely left my apartment and easily convinced Biggy to deliver my cookies ($1000 worth, about the size and thickness of a Fudge Stripes cookie, hence the symbolism) since he already knew better than anyone that it wasn't safe for me to drive anymore, and being the always-aiming-to-please dope pusher that he was, he made regular special deliveries of my cookies to my doorstep at no extra charge. What a guy! Talk about customer service!

By this time, I was so paranoid of the outside world (anything outside of my apartment) that any kind of light, including daylight, affected me like water to the Wicked Witch of the West in the *Wizard of Oz*. I kept my curtains and drapes drawn and allowed darkness to be my canopy, my new best friend. I'd only take the five-minute walk to the liquor store to restock after sundown, but once a week in broad daylight, I'd have to summon the courage to drive to the bank to cash the checks I was withdrawing from my retirement fund to pay Biggy. Shoot, if I had only made him the beneficiary of my account, I probably wouldn't have had to face the light at all. Who knew? I just wasn't thinking clearly, I suppose.

It had gotten so bad that I even stopped taking Teddy for his daily walks. I would just crack open the door wide enough for him to squeak out and allow him enough line from the retractable leash to get to the bottom of the steps to do his business, then I'd quickly yank him back up the steps and in the door. Poor Teddy. Some days, if I didn't feel like being inconvenienced, I wouldn't even allow him the privilege of going outside at all. I would just let him crap in the spare bedroom. What did it matter? No one ever visited me, and I was going to be moving on to the next world shortly anyway.

Teddy's Overdose

Some extremely crazy things happened between August 2005 (when my wife left) and February 6, 2007. I had nearly always partied alone. Whether it was drinking, weed, pills, cocaine, or crack, it was always just Teddy, me, and the demon.

Obviously, losing my family was a resounding number one, followed by the loss of my job and dozens of near fatal overdoses. However, there was also a terribly horrible incident involving Teddy during possibly the most horrific nine-month-cocaine/crack binge in the history of rock stars that nearly ended up being the most heartbreaking nightmare of them all.

Teddy had to witness behavior that should only be reserved for the devil himself. Prescription pills had turned me into a zombie and caused me to lose my job and family, but it was the return of my most powerful demon, cocaine, that had brought me to the verge of losing my very life and soul in my mid-twenties and again in my mid-forties.

Since I had now completely stopped listening to my "best Friend" and had absolutely no concept of a conscious anymore, God Himself reached down from heaven and used a ten-pound Pomeranian as an instrument to try and stop me from perishing forever.

Very much like my wife and my sons, Teddy could always sense when I was high, and it bothered him terribly.

It was during the episodes of my second go-around with the Iceman that Teddy began jumping into my lap and licking my face excessively in an effort to show his love and overt the madness. When I'd continually shove him back down to the floor, he'd jump back up on our couch and, lying down, would put his teddy bear-like face between his front paws and stare at me, shaking, with his eyes filled with tears and fear. Like the rest of those who loved me, Teddy tried pleading with me to stop the abuse.

It was during my powder cocaine spree up in Jersey between May 2006 and my departure to Florida in October that year that he would often knock my stash (pile of cocaine) off my coffee table whenever I'd leave the room or even just turn my head for a moment. I'd yell and scream at that poor little dog to "knock it off", but he was determined to go to great lengths to save me from myself.

The nightmare occurred in early December 2006. I had just gotten home from picking up a fresh cookie and promptly laid it on the coffee table in my living room. I then went to the kitchen to get a glass of red wine, which had become my normal ritual to kick-start a crack party. When I returned to the living room, the cookie was gone except for a few crumbs that were lying on the floor next to the table.

My dear almighty God! In a courageous effort to knock the monkey off my back once and for all, Teddy had gone on a kamikaze-like suicide mission and had eaten nearly an ounce (twenty-eight grams) of crack cocaine! Please note that a mere gram of cocaine is enough to kill an elephant.

As he began shaking horribly, I held him tightly in my arms and cried out to God, "Please don't let him die! Please don't let him die!" His horrified little brown eyes were bulging so badly that I feared they might pop out of his head! I could see his heart beating through his now rock-hard little chest, and he agonizingly squealed, trying desperately to catch his breath. He squealed and squealed, and I continued to cry, kiss him, hold him tightly, and repeatedly begged God, "Please don't let him die! I'll never do this again! Please God, don't let him die!"

I was panicking! I didn't know what to do! If I called 911, what would I tell them? That my dog had eaten my crack cocaine? I feared being arrested and going to jail more than watching my beloved partner die a horrible death right in my arms. I was soon to begin my out-patient drug program sentence for the November crack possession charge. Another felony dope charge would surely send me "up the road" (prison).

What could I do? I couldn't just let him die. He had just literally attempted to sacrifice his own life for me. This dog had stayed faithfully by my side during the most unquestionably trying period of my life. Then it hit me! Make him throw up! I quickly put him down and ran to the kitchen fridge. All I had was a gallon of milk, so I poured him a bowl, and he desperately gulped it down. I poured another and another until Teddy had polished off the entire gallon. It was as if he understood exactly the only remedy that would save his life, and it did. He began throwing up profusely! I picked him back up and held him close in my arms with his face pressed against mine. As I sobbed and kissed him on the head, I could see his eyes slowly begin to return to their normal size, the trembling ceased, and his breathing slowly returned to normal. It was absolutely a miracle. He was going to make it.

Just as it had happened countless times before when God had answered my petitions to spare my own life from overdoses, He again heard me and spared the life of my brave little pal. Out of overwhelming relief, I repeatedly praised God and went to bed that night, trying to grasp the significance of what had just happened.

The Divorce Papers

Although my wife and I had only been officially separated for a month and a half and were basically living in two completely different stratospheres, we were still dating and making a last-ditch effort to reconcile. At least that's what my completely obliterated heart and mind were telling me anyway. I mean, she couldn't have really given up on me, could she? "Till death do us part," right? Although I had quit on myself well over a decade ago, I honestly never could fathom her throwing the white towel into the ring. If love is blind, then I seriously needed a seeing eye dog. She had already moved on as far as our relationship was concerned, but I wasn't anywhere near ready to give up on my trophy.

Once the divorce had been finalized and before the ink was even dry, I realized that her promise of "starting all over again like when we were young" was all hogwash, fashioned to get me to sign the divorce papers (unaware of what they were, she had charmed me into signing some papers from her attorney during lunch one day at a local restaurant) quickly before I'd catch wind of her real intentions. I was never served the divorce papers or advised of a court appearance and only found out that our bond had been irrevocably broken when the news arrived quietly in my mailbox a week before Christmas. Although later I would completely understand her reasoning to sever our ties quickly, my heart was still unable to accept it.

Then as our once habitual phone conversations abruptly began to cease, I felt more and more like a lion who had lost his cub. Yes, I had been lied to. Yes, I had been deceived, but who could possibly blame her? There was no way she could have saved me. How can you change someone who can't change himself nor has the power or will to even attempt to? The fact that that poor sweet young lady had been butting heads with the devil himself for so long and still had the courage and strength to stand on her own was an absolute testament to the strength of her character.

So, how could I have expected a petite 105-lb. woman to defeat a monster that had already devoured the soul of her once indestructible husband? The fight was over, and this was only mere confirmation that our once perfect marriage and *Happy Days* family were undoubtedly gone forever.

It seemed that there was nothing that could possibly interfere with the date I had made with that pole on Fowler. No amount of crack was going to change that, but at least a cookie would make me delusional enough to avoid the reality of the catastrophic collapse of what was once an American dream of a life.

Teddy Runs Away

Late one night, as I was enjoying some weed and crack, I had a knock on my door. As I slowly cracked the door slightly open (in case it was the police, as if they wouldn't smell the aroma of crack in the air), it happened to be Willie's brother looking for him. As soon as Teddy heard something outside, he bolted through the door like Walter Payton, avoiding Willie's brother as if he were a would-be tackler. He went down the steps like a bat outta hell and off into the night. I was screaming for him at the top of my lungs while shoving Willie's brother out of my way as I stumbled down the steps in pursuit.

It was pitch dark, and Teddy was nowhere to be found. Except for Teddy's crack overdose, I can't ever remember being so scared. We were in a new neighborhood, and Teddy was only acquainted with the grounds around my building as I never took him for walks very far. I was running around the hood, terrified, yelling at the top of my lungs for my beloved best friend and angel. He was nowhere to be found, so I ran back home, jumped in my car, and drove all around the neighborhood with my car window down, yelling his name. It was so dark out that he could have been directly in front of me, and I would have never seen my little Pomeranian partner. I searched the area for hours, driving up and down the blocks, crying profusely, desperately hunting for my poor little dog until I finally gave up hope and went back to my hellhole in anguish.

My whole life, even before Jesus, I always felt that if I cried loud enough and hard enough, God would hear me and come to my rescue, and even as a woeful lost sinner, He always did. Romans 5:8 says that "God demonstrated His love for us, in that even while we were still sinners Christ died for us." He certainly showed His love for this pathetic sinner over and over again . . . If only I had not taken His love for granted, I could have saved myself and my family an awful lot of heartache.

Oh, the mercy and grace of God. He had no business loving me, but He did.

Philippians 4:6 says to "pray with supplication," which means to beg hard. I had never read that Scripture before that night, but I assure you I was begging God with every ounce of my being for Him to bring my sweet little friend back home. And even though I promised God for the trillionth time that I'd change my ways if He'd help me once again, after much bellowing and slobbering on my pillow, I went to sleep alone that night without my buddy lying next to me as he always had been.

In the morning, I staggered outta bed. I barely had the strength to stand, weakened from the events of the night before. I slowly opened the door to take one last hopeless look outside, and there he was . . . Teddy . . . sitting on my porch, smiling, and wagging his tail. I picked him up into my arms, squeezed him, and kissed his little face like never before. I once again cried out to God and praised Him for His goodness and faithfulness.

I'm tearing up at the remembrance of this story as well as the remembrance of the countless number of times that God showed up miraculously on my behalf. He saved me from countless overdoses. He saved Teddy from the crack overdose, and now He answered my cry once again and brought him home.

How many times does God have to humble and rescue a person before they will finally submit to Him and give in to His will for their life? We would soon find out.

She Laid Down the Law

Every now and then, an old piece of my soul would surface, and I would put down my pipe for an afternoon and drive downtown to see my now ex-wife and the kids. Then, during one of my guest appearances at their townhouse, she drew a line in the sand and angrily stated, "You can't just show up here whenever you want to, Dave! We aren't married anymore!" Wow! Talk about having your bubble burst. I guess I wouldn't be moving in there anytime soon.

Here I had no idea who I was anymore, and now I didn't know who my ex was either.

I yelled back, "I could care less what that piece of paper says (divorce settlement)! We're still married and always will be!" That's how I honestly felt inside. I was so out of touch with reality that the divorce felt kind of like a bad dream or bad trip, that's all. I would soon wake up, let the dust settle to find out it was just another illusion. I'd tell her how sorry I was again and talk her into making up, as I always had, and we'd march on. However, it was real, very real, or as D.J. had barked at me during or after one of my recent binges, "You've lost the one and only woman who was willing to put up with your crap (not exactly the adjective he used)!" Even hearing that from my beloved firstborn, who had been one of my biggest supporters, still wasn't enough to open my eyes to the fact that what was happening was not just another bad dream.

Boy, oh boy! All of that messing up and making up seemed endless to me, but I can't even imagine what the roller-coaster rides must have felt like to the former love of my life, who endured them with a clear, sober head. Ever wake up from a nightmare, then go back to sleep, and it picks up again right where you left off? Yeah, that's what our marriage must have seemed like to her. She would confess to me many years later when discussing the agony, "I'll never forget it," whereas I, the instigator, the abuser, often blacked out for days and couldn't recall a thing. Actually, there were some years that just completely disappeared off the radar screen. How convenient blackouts are for the perpetrator.

I would mess up real bad, hurt my wife real bad, then cry to her how sorry I was. "I'll never do it again! I promise!" I would buy her some flowers and kiss up for a few days, maybe even string together a good stretch for a couple of weeks on occasion. Then, the demons inside would coerce me into believing things were okay again, even back to normal, whatever our definition of normal may have been. I'd schmooze her over and again regain her trust, only to jump off the cliff again as soon as I had climbed back to the top. This pattern of erratic behavior happened continually for the greater part of twenty years but certainly reached a pinnacle the last ten years or so that we lived together.

I had quit many, many times, as I suppose all addicts can boast. I remember my high school freshman baseball coach Mr. McNellis, who also doubled as a brutal drunk and chain smoker. He used to joke, "Quitting is the easiest thing in the world! I've done it hundreds of times!" God rest his soul. I would learn firsthand, decades later, that Mr. Mac's joke wasn't at all funny.

My Spouse Had Moved On

A short while after she had so kindly reminded me that we were now divorced, I was compelled to call her one night during the week. I suppose you could call it a jealous ex-husband's intuition. When my calls and text messages went unanswered, as had become the norm, I called Adam. When he answered, I abruptly asked him to put his mother on the phone. He replied, "She's not home. She went to a concert at the Amalie Arena with the girls from work." Fine, no harm, no foul. That explained why she probably had her phone off. Yet, something was still giving me butterflies in my gut, so I put on my Sherlock Holmes hat and called the Arena.

When I found out the concert had been over for a couple of hours (it was now after midnight), I called her again, and again, no answer. I proceeded to call Adam again, and again, he confirmed she wasn't home yet. I smelled a rat! I was becoming completely whacked, bipolar to the max! One minute, I'd call her and leave a message, saying, "It's okay, I understand." Then, the next minute, I was pacing my apartment like a lion in a cage.

The following morning, she called me and explained that she had left her phone in the car that night after the concert, which is why she didn't return my calls. One thing about my ex: she had never been as good of a liar as I was. She would always get very defensive and raise her eyebrows when she told a fib. Although I couldn't see her eyebrows, she was certainly being defensive, which spurred me to take a drive downtown to her bank and pay her a visit.

When I arrived at her office, I began drilling her like F. Lee Bailey about the concert and why it took her so long to get home afterward.

However, before she could say, "I went out to eat with the girls afterward," her eyes opened wide, her eyebrows hit the roof, and the cat was out of the bag. I asked her if she had gone to the concert with a man, and sensing her alibi had been blown, she fessed up. She said, "He was just a customer at the bank, that's all." Oh no, she didn't! Not the old, "just a customer at the bank" line again! That's exactly the same line she used nine years earlier when I uncovered the "Chuck thing."

The Entanglement

Oh, the Chuck thing. It was the summer of 1997 when I experienced the deepest heartbreak I'd ever experienced next to the miscarriage of our first baby. It was a Saturday morning when I called her bank to chat. She worked a lot of half days on Saturday mornings and then would often go shopping afterward, or at least that's what I was led to believe. When I called the bank, they said she wasn't there, which was often the case when I'd call her at work on a Saturday morning. She said they would often send her to another branch that was busier and needed help.

For whatever reason, my jealous husband antennae were twitching strangely. A lot of things had happened during that season of our marriage that drew some suspicion. Trips to the grocery store took several hours, only to have her return home with only a gallon of milk and the excuse that she had run into her aunt or some other friend at the store, and they "just got to talking." There were several instances when she didn't realize I was in the next room and could hear her whispering on the phone, and then she'd abruptly hang up as soon as I entered the room. She was leaving a trail of breadcrumbs that would have made Hansel and Gretel proud but only led me down a road of suspicion that possibly my greatest fear may be much more than just suspicion.

On this particular morning, I noticed she showered, shaved her legs, and put on a skin-tight black mini-skirt. She looked more like she was going to a club or another infamous "concert with the girls" than going to work as a teller at a bank. I suppose that it was the image of the mini-skirt in my jealous head that caused my heart to beat uncontrollably when I inquired and was informed that she wasn't working at her normal location.

For whatever reason, I immediately suspected the worst. My hands were shaking uncontrollably as I called branch after branch, only to be informed at each inquiry that she wasn't there. Still unable to believe that my worst nightmare could be unfolding right before my eyes, I called her boss, something that my wife had specifically warned me to never do.

In my effort not to get her in trouble, I informed her boss that I was very sorry to bother her but that I had a family emergency and needed to talk to my wife. She seemed alarmed that I didn't know she wasn't scheduled to work. As I apologized again and hung up, I was on the verge of a panic attack. I was shaking and sweating, then at that very moment, something inside me reminded me that I had not seen a cell phone bill in quite some time.

My wife was our family accountant, paid the bills, and was meticulous at it. She kept all the bills perfectly organized in a shoe box. I sought out the shoebox, then quickly started fumbling through it. Everything was in perfect order except for one thing: there were no cell phone bills. I immediately called the phone company and informed them that I had not received a bill from them in quite a while. They told me that my wife had called and asked them to send the bills to her bank. I couldn't breathe upon hearing that. I was literally terrified, then asked them to fax me copies of all the bills to my job, but even before receiving them, I felt like I had been stabbed in the heart. Let's just say it was my jealous husband's intuition, which should have been alerted years before but now had me shaking uncontrollably. There was no logical explanation why my wife would have changed the mailing address except for one: she was trying to hide something. I didn't even need to see the phone bills to know that my wife had committed the unforgivable sin, and I'm not referring to blasphemy of the Holy Spirit (Luke 12:10), if you know what I mean.

We only had one cell phone back then, and it was my dumb idea that my wife hold onto it for safety purposes just in case her car broke down or something. She worked quite a ways from home, whereas I worked just a few miles up the road. I remember just sitting there on the couch in our TV room, feeling paralyzed with fear, waiting for her to get home so I could interrogate her. Never in all my wildest dreams would I have ever expected my soulmate to be unfaithful; this just couldn't be possible . . . There must be some logical explanation, yet every possible scenario kept leading to her and some snake doing the wild thing at his crib . . . at hotels . . . in his car, and so on.

The devil is known for his wiles; however, it appeared this was no trick he was playing. There was absolutely nothing I could do but wait for what seemed like an eternity for the once love of my life to arrive home from another hard day at work. When she finally got home, she found me still sitting upstairs in the TV room with a look of horrible disbelief. I asked her to sit down, then hit her with the million-dollar question, "Where were you today?"

She quickly replied, "At work." I told her I called the office, and they said she wasn't there. And she gave her usual stock reply, "Oh, they sent me to such and such branch." Instantly, her eyebrows raised, and she was busted. I told her I talked to her boss, and she said she had off, and before she could come up with another story, I went for the kill shot. "Where are the cell phone bills?" She went and got the shoebox and put on an amazing Oscar winning performance. She started fumbling through the box just I had done earlier before I halted her.

"I already talked to the phone company, and they're faxing me all the bills. She knew the charade was over. She put down her head and started crying. I calmly asked her for the cell phone, and she promptly handed it to me. I got up and went downstairs to the garage, found my favorite hammer, and bashed it to pieces. I then picked up all the pieces and walked back upstairs and calmly handed her the pieces and said, "Now make your calls!" I went into the bathroom and sat on the toilet and cried my eyes out. She came in and sat in front of me and asked me if I wanted her to leave, and I just shook my head no.

When I got the bills the next day and began analyzing them, it was much worse than I had anticipated. Except for our home number, there was only one other phone number on all the bills, so I bravely—change that—I anxiously and angrily called it. I wanted blood, man . . . you know, OPP . . . You don't mess with other people's property, and my wife was my property. I wanted to confront that SOB; however, all I got was an answering machine.

"Hello, it's Chuck . . . I'm not home right now . . ." He quickly had his number changed, and I never got the satisfaction of bashing his head in just like I had the cell phone.

She said they were just friends and had never slept together, and since I had no evidence or eyewitness accounts to the contrary, I wanted that to be true so badly. We stayed together and tried so hard to communicate our way through, and although she apologized and reiterated that it was only a friendship, and I said I forgave her, I realized that it wasn't until 2/7/07 that I truly forgave her in my heart.

The problem is whether it's a relationship with your spouse, your employer, or God, trust is everything, and when it's broken, the relationship is terribly hard to repair. I even apologized to her at the time. I told her it was all my fault. If I had taken care of business as a husband and treated her the way she should have been treated, she would have never required a secret friend.

The whole situation had humbled me. I remember Jesus saying in Matthew 7:24–27,

> A wise man builds his house upon a rock and when the rains and winds come and beat on that house it will not fall because it's built on the rock. But a foolish man builds his house on the sand and when the rain and winds descended and the floods came the house fell, and great was its fall.

Great was its fall, huh? Yeah, that's a pretty perfect way to describe it, Jesus. I was that fool, and my house had just come tumbling down. If only I had followed the promptings God had placed on my heart from childhood and been the godly man, son, brother, husband, and father I was always called to be and had built my house on the rock of Christ, well, who knows how differently our family may have turned out. I took the blame then, and I take it till this day.

I Wasn't Saved

During another specially heated argument with my wife, I pulled out the adulteress card once again, as I often did when she was winning, and reminded her that she would be going to hell because of her entanglement.

She snarled at me, "Oh, like you're going to heaven or something?"

I assured her, "I know I'm going to heaven!" I had always assumed I was. After all, I had believed in God and prayed to God every day since childhood. However, I didn't understand at the time that head knowledge was much different than heart knowledge. I always knew there was a God, surely because of His prevenient grace (Titus 2:11) that had always been tugging at my heart just like it does at everyone's heart at some point. However, as Romans 10:9 says, "that if you confess with your mouth the Lord Jesus and believe in your heart that God has raised Him from the dead, you will be saved."

I didn't have a personal relationship with Jesus, and if I had died during any one of my over one hundred overdoses before 2/7/07, I would have been that guy who stood at the gate, saying, "Lord, Lord," and Jesus would have said, "I never knew you; depart from me . . ." (Matt. 7:21-23), and I would have spent all eternity in the outer darkness of hell, completely separated from God's presence forever.

The sad thing is that I kept calling her an adulteress, yet I had actually no proof that she was. She said that Chuck was a good listener, insinuating that I wasn't, and she was right. We lived together, but I was never there mentally and certainly didn't want to hear about overdrafts at the bank or any of her other concerns, for that matter. I figured that I worked and always came home afterward and never took part in the weekend poker games with the guys, so that justified my innocence before God. Oh, please!

Sex was another of my addictions . . . and possibly my greatest weakness. On Friday nights, my wife worked late at the bank, and that gave me a window of opportunity to satisfy my lusts. The guys from work and I would sneak out of work early and head to the go-go bars ten minutes away, but that was okay, right? It was a guy thing to grab a few beers to burn off some steam after a hard week of work, right? And having a few lap dances in the back room with the girls was completely fine, right? After all, we weren't having sex or anything. Wow . . . I was so guilty.

If only I had known Jesus and had heard what He had said in Matthew 5:28 that "anyone who even looks at a woman to lust for her has already committed adultery with her in his heart." Well, isn't that quite the revelation? I was an adulterer long before my wife ever was (if she even was), and if she was going to hell, I was certainly going to be the one personally welcoming her into the lake of fire.

God is a just God and warns us about an "eye for an eye," so as it turned out, I got exactly what I had coming to me, and those twenty-dollar dances extracted a huge toll on my soul and my marriage.

We Renewed Our Vows

We had been through so many trials over the course of our marriage, and even through all of it, we tried so hard to always work it out.

On January 17, 1998, we even renewed our marriage vows just before sunset on Queen Elizabeth's yacht out in the Caribbean Sea off the coast of Negril, Jamaica.

It was an amazing week at the all-inclusive Grand Lido Resort. It included a complete hair, nails, and makeup makeover for her, a wedding cake, unlimited champagne, a sunset cruise, a candlelit dinner for two, and all the trimmings, all paid for by SuperClubs (true story) in response to one of my letters written about how disappointing our family's stay was at their Boscobel Beach Resort a couple years prior, which, of course, was a complete scam made up by yours truly.

After we had returned home, she left a beautiful "Thank You" card for me to find on the front seat of my car. It read, "Thank you so much for such a beautifully planned vacation. You made me feel like the only woman on the whole island. I love you!"

The Restraining Order

When I marched angrily into her office at work the day after her concert venture and learned she was already dating someone, it didn't matter to me that we weren't officially married anymore (although I had a marriage certificate from our Jamaica trip that said we were), and when she humbly explained, with her head bowed, that she "had just met him," her hole was getting deeper and deeper.

We had only been divorced for six weeks after twenty-four years of marriage. How could she possibly be going to a concert with a man she just met and then stay out until after midnight in the middle of the week with my teenage son home alone? Man, oh man, did I erupt! I screamed, "How could you do this to me again after you knew how badly it broke my heart the first time!"

I forgave her for the first indiscretion because I simply couldn't imagine living without her, but that David existed no more. The new, and certainly not improved David, had obviously just been dumped by his former wife for some low-life predator, and he wanted blood! Not hers, although it certainly takes two to tango, but the "sugar daddy," the "silver-tongued devil" who had preyed on her during the most vulnerable period of her life, the guy who slithered in like the snake in Eden and convinced her that it was okay to have her fruit and eat it too. I never did like snakes, especially ones who fool around with married women.

I was boiling! I began ranting and raving, and she warned me, "Keep it down! You're gonna get me fired!" I told her I was going to "find out who it was, track him down, and beat him over the head with a baseball bat!" Oops, not a good choice of words in the light of all the attention O. J. Simpson had brought to domestic violence in previous years.

Although I had never laid a hand on my wife, nor anyone else for that matter, I could see her becoming frightened by my demeanor. Heck, I was frightened by it. She was beginning to stutter and advised me, "Ca-ca-ca-calm down, or I'm gonna get a re-re-restraining order!"

I fired back, "Yeah, you may wanna do that!" I continued to vent, but having blacked out from my anger, I don't remember what else was said, nor do I remember anything I did immediately after stomping out of her office. I do remember, though, an officer called me the following afternoon and left a message on my cell phone to contact him immediately. When I did, he informed me he had "papers" to serve me and needed to meet with me right away. I danced around the issue and told him I "wasn't going to be around." It was Friday, and I told him I had "plans to go to Miami for the Super Bowl that weekend." I informed him that my brother was there working for NFL Films, and I was going to spend a few days with him.

Most of that was true except for the part about me leaving town. I had no intentions of going anywhere. I spent that weekend drinking and chain smoking crack as fast as I could load up my tin foil pipe and suck it down. I did watch the Super Bowl but could not tell you who played, who won, or anything else about it. I was in a very bad place, a state of mind and darkness that can only be described with one word: hell. It's like I was outside of my body, just standing there and witnessing something so dreadful that even I could barely watch. One hit after another, all night long, with my thumb sore and burnt from flicking the lighter over and over again to ignite another "rock"; this is what my life had become, just one long "hit."

Then, when I finally laid my head on my pillow, right before dawn, there was a knock on my door. I figured it was probably Willie trying to escape his wife, as he often did by ducking upstairs to my place, but when I opened the door, much to my surprise, it was an officer, or server, as they are called. I quickly understood, to my great relief, that he wasn't there to arrest me but to "serve" me a restraining order that my ex-wife had taken out right after my tantrum at her office. The guy was talking and explaining the thing to me in detail, but I was in a daze and wasn't hearing a word.

When he finally left, I simply threw the papers on my coffee table and went to bed, kind of like how a vampire goes to his coffin before sunup. I didn't sleep very long, though. I mean, how could I, with all the chaos that was going on in my quagmire of a life? I quietly and peacefully sat down in my favorite armchair and began reading the restraining order. The more I read, the more I got upset. I was ordered not to come within one hundred yards of my ex, her job, or her house and to have absolutely no contact of any kind with her for a period of one week. That was all fine and dandy, but when I got to the part that also ordered me to stay away from my son Adam, well, that just sent me overboard. I immediately picked up the phone and called her to voice my displeasure. When I questioned the whole idea of taking out a restraining order against me when she knew I never had, nor ever would harm her, even in my worst drug-induced state, she defended her decision by saying, "There's always a first time for everything. And you told me to do it!" Oh yeah, I guess I did.

When I questioned her further about not being able to see Adam, she argued that she hadn't said that, even though I was reading it in black and white, and it had been signed by her. She promptly said, "It's only for a week, and if you behave yourself, then we'll take it from there." She then texted me and promised to call me later to discuss the whole matter that evening. Well if to God, "a day is like a thousand years" (2 Pet. 3:8), then to me, a week without seeing or talking to my better half, well, that was like an eternity.

I thought about her, that guy, my sons, and a million other things all at once. Since I was way too wired to wait even a few hours for our proposed meeting that evening, I hopped into my car and started driving downtown to her bank on Davis Island. When I got there, I circled the part in the restraining order that pertained to Adam and left it slipped under the windshield wiper on her car. I then parked a short way down the street, well, outside the one-hundred-yard limit but well within eyesight of the bank, and waited anxiously for her reaction.

When she finally came out after work, I could see her standing in the middle of the parking lot, looking all around. I assumed she was looking for me, so I turned on my car and drove over to confront her. When I did, it certainly wasn't a welcome surprise.

She nervously said, "You're not supposed to be here, Dave! You gotta leave!"

Then, trying to break the ice and schmooze her over, I smiled and asked, "How do you like my new haircut?"

Without barely even looking at me, she responded, "Yeah, it looks nice; now you gotta go."

When I attempted to defend my actions and pressed the issue about the restraining order, she threatened to call the police. When I continued pressing, she dialed the phone, but apparently it wasn't the police she called since the only one who showed up was a short, stocky, older, mafia-looking dude from around the corner. I would find out a year later that this was her new "friend."

He began waving his fist at me and threatened me to "get the f--- outta here!" I thought for an instant about getting out of my car and pounding his head into the parking lot, which I certainly would have done if I had known at the time who he was, but instead, I tried appealing to her one more time by yelling out my window, "I love you!" Then, fearing that the police might be on their way, I quickly drove out of Dodge.

Although I made it back to my apartment safely, everything in my world was moving like an out-of-control roller coaster. I was so confused and filled with anxiety that I didn't even drink or get high that evening, which was extremely abnormal for me. Instead, I spent it repeatedly calling and texting her. I had to talk to her. I had to fix this. There was no need for a restraining order. All she had to do was go back downtown, have it lifted, and then we'd work this thing out.

I waited, I texted, and I called, but no response from her. Then, it finally sunk into my mush-like head that she had again reneged on a promise and had no intention of "talking it over" that night. I was really, really tired of being played like a fool! I was left with no other recourse. If she wasn't going to at least show me the courtesy of a call-back, then I would have to go see her face-to-face. Yeah, there was a restraining order, but she did say that we were going to "talk it over" that evening, so a surprise visit seemed justified. Boy, oh boy, were my insides churning as I raced downtown with Teddy resting comfortably in the passenger seat.

I could hear the good angel and the bad angel arguing within my head. The good angel said, "Don't go over there, David! You'll be making a big mistake!" While the bad angel said, "Go ahead, David. Go talk to her; it'll be okay. You can work this out."

All the way over there during the twenty-minute drive, the good angel and the bad angel battled for control of my will. There was truly a fierce battle being fought within my head, and to make matters even worse, if that's possible, I couldn't distinguish which voice was which. One minute, I wanted to turn around and go back home, then the next minute, I was flooring the gas pedal like Mario Andretti. It was a long twenty-minute ride filled with contemplation.

How did a marriage made in heaven turn into a train wreck? What caused me to become such an angry, disgruntled, miserable man, whose wife wished he were dead and despised him so badly that she wanted to scratch his eyes out? Who had become so disgusting to her that she had recently informed him that he was the "last person in the world" she would ever sleep with, a man who hated himself, the world, and everything in it?

When I finally arrived at the exclusive Harbour Island gated community where my family resided, security stopped me at the entrance, and since my name had been removed from the visitor's list, I was denied entry. No problem, I simply parked my car around the corner and then walked right past the same guard shack into the development like a senior citizen on a Sunday stroll. (IMAGE 4)

It certainly appeared that the couple of hundred bucks my ex was being raked for Homeowner Association fees, which included security, could have been much better spent.

As I approached her house, I could see her car in the driveway, and several of the houselights still on. I had called to let her know I was coming, so I assumed she was expecting me. I knocked on the front door several times, but there was no answer. I knew that she and Adam were inside since it was getting late (approximately 10 p.m.), and it was a school night. I phoned her again, but my efforts were in vain. I was getting frustrated and began knocking harder. I was determined to plead my case to her.

Finally, after several minutes, she came to the door but refused to open it. She screamed through the door, "What do you want?"

I answered, "Please let me in so we can talk!"

She screamed again, "I just want you to go away!"

I was crying as I told her, "I'm sorry. I was never mad at you. I was mad at myself and took it out on you."

I had realized during the drive over there that I had been so disappointed in myself for so long because I had always wanted to do the right thing but lacked the fortitude to repent and make the necessary changes to become the husband and father I knew inside I was always meant to be.

I knew that what I was doing was wrong, and although I only hated myself subconsciously and meant only to punish myself, I was also destroying my entire family.

Only an addict can understand the pain and hopelessness of dwelling in a body that's completely void of self-control; the purgatory of being on the outside looking in, and although detesting what you see, being powerless to do anything about it.

Before I had the opportunity to explain to her any further, all heck broke loose. It looked like a 4th of July celebration right there in my family's driveway, with all the different color flashing lights and screaming sirens. I'm not sure how many police cars there were, but they appeared out of nowhere and lit up the entire street. My goodness; you would have thought they had found Osama bin Laden right there in downtown Tampa.

The 2nd Arrest in Florida

The officer informed me that I was under arrest and read me my rights, just like I had seen so many times on TV. The only difference is that this was real life, my life. I politely asked him if he would ask my ex-wife if she really wanted me to go to jail, but before he could politely reply, "We have no choice. You broke the law," I felt something that I'll never forget. The feeling of cold, hard handcuffs as the officer cuffed my hands behind my back. He then opened the back door of what must have been the smallest police car on the face of the earth. Talk about having a bad day. I was clueless about how to get in with my hands cuffed behind me and absolutely no legroom between the seats. He obliged me by lowering me into the car onto my side as I wiggled myself across the seat to get my feet inside.

As I lay there on my back with my hands cuffed underneath me, I writhed in pain! The cuffs were so hard and tight! I thought for sure they were going to break my wrists. I kept squirming around like a worm on a hook, trying to find a position of comfort, which I never did achieve. All I could think about, except for the unbearable pain from the cuffs, was my poor son Adam having to watch his dad being arrested. He must have been so scared, much more so than myself, since he was still capable of experiencing emotion, whereas I was no longer capable of feeling anything.

Boy, when God wants to send you a wake-up call, He sure doesn't mess around. The officer shut my door, then went inside my family's house for what seemed like forever, the same house that was paid for from the money I had graciously given to her as part of our divorce settlement and the house I believed wholeheartedly that I'd be moving into after we had one day reconciled. "There is a way that seems right to a man, but its end is the way of death" (Prov. 16:25). How our best-laid plans sometimes go awry, huh?

When he finally returned and got into the car, he interrogated me about the messages I had left on my ex's phone. I admitted I had placed a "few calls," but he said there were twenty-three, and he listened to every one of them and recited verbatim the ones that were especially nasty toward her. Oops, but cut me a break. She promised we were going to talk that night, then ignored all my calls. What was I supposed to do? Yeah, there was a restraining order, but . . .

The station at Orient Road Jail was only about fifteen minutes away, so why was it taking forever to get there? By now, I had to go to the bathroom so bad that my liver was hurting almost as bad as my wrists. When I informed the officer, "I gotta go bad!" he replied, "We'll be there soon." He then promptly pulled into a dark vacant lot and began filling out his report.

As I continued to flop around like a fish on dry land in the back seat with my bowels about to explode, Barney Fife diligently searched through his law book for every possible charge but the kitchen sink to throw at me. When I asked him if I'd be going home tomorrow, he said, "I don't know. These are some pretty serious charges."

I sarcastically questioned, "You gotta be kidding me! I got pissed at my wife for fooling around on me, and I got to go to jail?"

However, before he could explain the seriousness of breaking a restraining order, two more police cars pulled up, and I began to feel like I was in *America's Most Wanted* or something. Were all the Dunkin Donuts closed, or what? Barney then got out of our car and, along with his gang of "Tampa's finest," spent well over an hour gossiping in the parking lot about the theory of relativity, their daughter's softball games, and other pertinent subjects.

Silly me, here I always thought cops did nothing but eat donuts and drink coffee while they were supposed to be hard at work. Because of the way things went down during my November arrest with Willie, I was left with a very sour taste in my mouth toward law enforcement, just in case you couldn't tell.

Poor Teddy at 2nd Arrest

Poor Teddy, the look of fear on his tiny, kind Pomeranian face as the officers removed him from my car the night of my arrest will be embedded in my mind forever. I deserved to be arrested, but Teddy didn't deserve any of this trauma. His only crime was his loyalty to his drug-infested owner. He undeservedly had to witness hell itself. Night after night, and coke binge after coke binge, he watched as I lay grasping the sides of my bed, much like a kid grasping the armrests on a roller coaster ride while observing my heart beating out of my chest. I would beg God over and over not to let me die. I remember the fear of my heart exploding as I promised Him I would stop if He would just give me another chance.

As I lay there alone, terrified, night after night, Teddy would always jump into the bed and lay right beside me. It's amazing how animals can sense when something is wrong or when we aren't feeling well and do their best to comfort us. Teddy would lick my left hand obsessively as my body twitched and shook from the drug coursing through my veins. Teddy was all I had, and I was all Teddy had, and he feared losing me as much as I feared being found dead by my sons or whoever else may have the unfortunate task of discovering my corpse. And although I would angerly push him away from me during and throughout each binge, I so much appreciated him always coming to my aid when the party was over and I was barely holding on for dear life. I also always appreciated God for giving me chance after chance to honor my fox-hole prayers, even though He knew darn well that I would renege on my vows the second the storm had passed, and I was fortunate enough to witness another sunrise.

Booking

W e finally made it to the jail approximately three hours later, a little after 1:00 a.m. For three hours, I lay in the dark of the back seat of that police car. It seemed like no matter where I went, darkness followed me like a shadow. I just couldn't escape it. Hmm, it was a very interesting representation of what my life had become as I look back.

The officer took me inside the station to be booked, and who would ever believe that the thought of getting a jail cell was actually sounding pretty comforting to me by then, maybe even giving me a sense of security from the demons that had been hawking me so hard for so long. I was unable to escape them on the outside, so possibly that steel cell door could keep them away.

It had been a very draining week, and to be honest, I was really just looking forward to lying down, even if it was on a cold, hard, steel bunk.

When you enter the jail for booking, they first get all your personal information, then take all your belongings to be held in property until your release. After that, you sit down and wait for your name to be called for fingerprinting, your mug shot, and your wrist ID band.

When they called my name for the picture, I remembered how my ex had eerily kept my mug shot from the previous arrest in her top desk drawer at her office. Kind of weird, I thought, since she had tons of pictures of me at home but chose to keep the very worst one of my life. In fact, that was the only one she had of me in her office. Bizarre. It appeared to be some kind of a trophy to her, the symbol of some morbid victory or something. I was never able to get an explanation for it, but remembering that and the fact that she would probably be searching the internet for this masterpiece as soon as it became available the next morning, I posed for the picture with my very best smiley face. Well, at least I thought I was smiling. However, I had dwelled in Zombie Land for so long that I couldn't even fake a smile anymore, even on the biggest of stages. I tried my darndest, though. You know me, Mr. Competitor. I couldn't allow her to think she had finally gotten the last laugh or smile, as it were. Man, what a sorry state of mind I had been reduced to.

Neither of us was smiling on this night, that's for certain. In fact, D.J. told me a couple of years later that my ex-wife had cried for months after my arrest, and in some morbid way, that actually made me feel good, thinking that she was possibly crying for me, or for us, or for what could've been, but now wasn't anymore. That secret may always remain between her and God.

After the mug shot, I had to sit and wait for my cell assignment. I guess it always pays to make reservations. The booking room was absolutely packed, standing room only, which I could understand if it was a Friday or Saturday, but it seemed unusual to me since it was a Tuesday night.

I had been so terrified during my first arrest and three-day stay at Club Orient Road in November that I hadn't realized how accommodating they are to the world's worst. They came around almost every hour handing out free food, compliments of the Florida taxpayers, and since I was renting and didn't pay taxes, this was a free meal in every sense of the word.

I shamefully admit that over the course of the fifteen to twenty hours that I was delayed in that booking room, spending much of it sleeping on the cold tile floor and humbly waiting for the luxury of a cell, I indulged in nine of the most delicious bologna and cheese sandwiches I've ever enjoyed, not to mention the lovely juice boxes that accompanied them. I ate so many bologna sandwiches that there's an outside chance that I may never eat another one again as long as I live. I believe it's the system's way of preparing the prisoners for the daily delicacies they'll receive from the Hillsborough County Sheriff's Office once they are finally situated within the jail walls.

What was taking them so long? It had been nearly a full day since I entered the confines, and people were coming in the door several hours after I had, yet had already been ushered off to a cell. Yet, there I lay, waiting and waiting. It was okay at first while I was stuffing myself full of pork, but now that I had my fill and almost felt like puking, the fun was over, and I seriously wanted my room.

First Night in Jail

When my number finally got called, and boy, oh boy, did it ever get "called," it was the evening of February 7, 2007. They proceeded to escort me into a changing room to strip me of everything else I had, including my dignity. They then gave me a whole new wardrobe consisting of crap-stained jail drawers, white socks, plastic slides, and a two-piece jumpsuit that was the ugliest orange I had seen since my first car, a Chevy Belair. It's been over seventeen years since I sported that putrid orange jumpsuit, but I can remember clearly having a distinct feeling that my life would never be the same again.

When a group of about a half dozen of us had changed and been assembled and were ready to be delivered to our new residences, we began the long walk, which ended at dorm 6b, or "Six Bravo," as it's referred to in jail talk. My new home would be cell 24, and although the Orient Road Jail consisted of single and double cells, I was given the added pleasure of being housed in a double with my new roomie Mike. Mike, as he later revealed to me, had brutally beaten his wife so bad that she lost an eye, and he cut up his friend with a box cutter when he had discovered them doing the wild thing in his bedroom one night after arriving home from work.

Was anything normal at all going to happen on this evening? First, my ex blew off our date, igniting my drive to doom, the cuffs and the bladder problem in the cramped back seat of the police car, the three-hour parking lot jaunt and a nearly twenty-four-hour wait for a cell, and then the grand finale: the less-than-pressed undies, hideous orange jumpsuit, and a cell with a lifetime criminal accused of not one but two attempted murders. They couldn't have let me shack up with a tax evader or a jaywalker? Oh no, that would have ruined this picture-perfect evening.

God was humbling me. It was as if after decades of resisting His purpose and plan for my life, He was putting me in such an uncomfortable position that I would finally choose to give in to His will. Although I seriously doubt He ever wanted me to become a felon, He will do what He has to do to break our spirits. Jesus said in Matthew 5:3, "Blessed are the poor in spirit for theirs is the kingdom of heaven." Well, I certainly wasn't feeling blessed, and I definitely was not in heaven.

"What in the world is going on here?" I pondered. "It's the Nightmare on Elm Street part 10! Someone's going to hear about this when I get out of here tomorrow," I thought. They certainly must not know about my writing skills.

Mike was a black man who wasn't to be mistaken as cordial and was in a foul mood when I unexpectedly showed up in his cell that night. It's one thing to be awakened from a blessed sweet jailhouse slumber but quite another to have some uninvited goofy cracker move into your crib. Mike clearly had made "6b48" his house, and I quickly sensed from the grumbling noises coming from him that he liked dwelling alone in that house.

Since my new buddy Mike had taken ownership of the preferred bottom bunk, I humbly climbed up onto the top one. As was the case with the rest of the previous twenty-four hours, nothing was going to go as I would have liked. My cold steel bunk included only a sheet. The standard jail cell amenities of a blanket and pillow had somehow been overlooked by the housekeeping staff. It was obviously additional fuel to be included in my letter to the governor. Oh, that's right, there was no housekeeping service in jail. The inmates were the housekeepers. It took me all of about two seconds to equate that this was not an "all-inclusive" jail I was frequenting.

Mike was a "trustee" (food server/preparer), I later learned, which meant our cell door was allowed to be left open, and that was actually quite a benefit. A trustee could go out and sit in the common area of the POD and watch TV and heat up some snacks while everyone else had to stay in their cells after lights out time.

Although he was asleep when I arrived that night, nature called him suddenly, and he wanted some quiet time to take a number two in his house (what a pleasant surprise; each cell has its own toilet). He promptly asked me to wait outside while he did his business. He was a tad shy, I guess. The accommodating house guest that I was, I obliged him by standing outside our cell door while he read the newspaper and "dropped the kids off at the pool." Like a dog relieving himself on a tree, Mike was marking his territory by making me stand there for the better part of twenty minutes. By the time I whispered through the doorway, "Are you done?" he was already tucked back into his bunk, sound asleep. Mike had a gift in that he could fall asleep the instant his head touched the pillow. It was a great gift to have, no doubt, especially when you've spent most of your adult life incarcerated.

When I finally climbed back into the momentary security of my bunk, the devil and his army were there waiting for me. It seems he wasn't going to let the jail cell walls interfere with the progression of his ultimate plan of destruction that he had laid out for me. Remember, my date with the pole on Fowler Avenue loomed only a week away before my ex's life-changing and soul-saving decision to band me from her life for a week.

Reality had set in, and my mind became flooded with horrible thoughts about where I was, what I had done, and where I was going to be for possibly a very long time. There was a good chance I was going to miss Adam's eighth grade and high school graduations and his games, along with D.J.'s college graduation, depending upon the outcome and severity of the charges to be brought against me.

Was this really happening to me? Was it really possible that my life could get even worse than it already was? There was now nowhere to go. I had been a master of escaping my messes for over 2-1/2 decades, but how was I possibly going to get out of this pit I had dug for myself? There was a pretty darn good chance that the sheriff wasn't going to pat me on the butt and say, "It's okay, kid; you can go home. Just don't let it happen again." Although, I honestly was hoping he would.

I had been "ripping and racing" for so long I didn't really know how to do anything else. I didn't know it was possible to slow down. I just figured that one day, the madness would run its course, I would grow up, stop running around like a child, begin behaving like an adult, and we'd live happily ever after. After all, that's what my ex and I did when problems arose; we ran from them.

We had moved from our Sunnybrook townhouse when D.J. was a couple of years old with the hope of escaping the Iceman, which we certainly did for a season. Yet, it didn't take long for newer and just as wily demons to consume me. We moved from Edgewater Park in an effort to halt my growing infatuation with the "juice demon," followed immediately by my growing thirst for the "liquor demon." Finally, we sold our new custom-built dream home in Burlington Township after only three years to hide from the "Oxycontin demon." Demon after demon, one by one, we attempted to flee, but they relentlessly trailed us, or me, I should say, like an ominous cloud, a cloud that was becoming darker and darker. Finally, an exhausted, broken woman mustered up the courage to flee from what had culminated into the biggest demon of them all, me.

Time to End It

I was completely alone, and there was now nowhere for me to run. I couldn't run from reality any longer, and that may have been the scariest reality of them all. There would be no more hiding in a pill, booze bottle, crack pipe, or somewhere within the darkness of my mind. So, what could I possibly do? I hadn't had to face reality head-on without my ex or the aid of chemicals since I was eighteen years old, and now that I was forty-six and had completely lost everything in my life, I certainly wasn't in the mindset to start. I was in a cold, dark jail cell, and it was time to "pay the piper," "to put up or shut up," to face the only thing that I had really been trying to avoid since that day in Henry's dorm room, my long lost "best Friend."

I was too ashamed to face Him. How could I? I had let Him down so terribly. I had abandoned Him for absolutely no good reason except that I liked to get high . . . I was addicted to pleasure. Heck, I loved it! I loved it more than my family, more than my job, more than my health, and certainly more than Him. But I needed Him now. I needed Him desperately.

As I pondered my situation and my options, my heart began pounding uncontrollably within my chest. How could I possibly live in there five to ten years without ESPN, without my better half and the kids, wearing other people's dirty underwear, and eating dog food? There was only one resolution, I couldn't. There was absolutely no way I could endure the heartache that engulfed me. I needed out. I wanted out. But how?

Since there were no sharp objects in jail, I couldn't slice my wrists. That would be too slow anyway, and besides, I hated blood. Then, the answer came to me, or should I say, the choice. I had heard about inmates hanging themselves and decided that was my only option. The jury of darkness within my head had spoken. The verdict was in. Death by hanging, and Lord knows, I was getting off easy for a lifetime of cowardliness and self-indulgence.

I was completely irrational and filled with dark, horrid thoughts. The idea of tying up a noose and wandering up to the second floor out of the sight of the deputy while the others slept to perform the dirty deed actually brought a sense of relief to me. The nightmare called my life could finally and quickly be concluded. Finally, I could find the freedom that my soul had been searching for what seemed like an eternity. They would find me hanging there from the top railing first thing in the morning. Yeah, that would fix them! Everyone who had ignored my pain and suffering and declined to show me any sympathy, as that was my normal mindset for so many years. I was hurting inside and wanted everyone else to hurt as well. Misery loves company, I suppose. After all, my boss never appreciated how hard I had worked all those years, my parents loved my brother more than me, and my wife, well, she had never appreciated any of my sacrifices for her or our family. I must have been the most underappreciated man who ever walked the face of the earth.

A common denominator with addicts is that their cowardice is the result of factors caused by everyone but themselves. Sadly, after countless attempts by my family and friends to try and help me, I also had convinced myself that my foolishness was the direct result of their lack of empathy when the truth was that a fool thinks foolish thoughts and says and does foolish things. A fool pretty much defined David S. Gaskill Sr. completely.

God's Word says, "God has chosen the foolish things of this world to put to shame the wise, and God has chosen the weak things of the world to put to shame the things which are mighty" (1 Cor. 1:27). "Well, let God be true and everyone else a liar" (Rom. 3:4).

I was certainly the weakest fool the Hillsborough County jail system had ever boarded, so if God's Word was true, He was gonna have to perform His greatest conversion since Apostle Paul on the road to Damascus (Acts 9).

The Shadow of Death

It didn't really matter at this point whose snare had led me to reach my darkest hour. All that mattered was that I was getting out of it, breaking free from the chains that had me bound my entire adult life. So, I sat there on my bunk with my buddy Mike, snoring like a diesel truck below me, and began fondling the sheet that I'd use as the weapon of mass destruction. As I held it in my hands, a different spirit came over me suddenly, and along with it, a deeper feeling of peace.

I looked at the sheet in my hands, trying to decipher how to make a noose, and my mind went blank . . . or maybe emptied would better describe it. I couldn't figure out how to make a noose for the life of me. I tried to recall how the cowboys in the old western movies tied up their lassos, yet I continued to draw a blank. I was twisting it, fighting with it, and sweating at my failure, and then something inside me peacefully said, "No. Not tonight. You're too tired." Jesus invited us in Matthew 11:28, "Come to Me, all you who labor and are heavy laden, and I will give you rest." Boy, was I tired, sick and tired, I mean, physically, mentally, and spiritually wiped out. Exhausted! So, I figured I would just lay down, go to sleep, sneak upstairs, and set myself free from the torment of this world the following night.

I still didn't have a pillow, so I folded up my towel and laid my head down. The very moment my head hit that makeshift pillow, a spirit of humility fell over me. Anxiety was again sneaking in the back door as my chest began pounding. "I'm going to miss Adam's high school games, D.J.'s college graduation, and maybe even their weddings! I'm going to miss everything!" I pondered. And just as I had done on so many other occasions in my life when I was filled with fear, I called on God for help.

"I'm in jail, man! I'm in freaking jail, and I may be here a long time!" I couldn't hold back my grief and began crying uncontrollably while attempting to smother my anguish in the towel as I lay there, pressed firmly against the cold white concrete wall. "I'm so sorry! I'm so sorry. I pissed away all the blessings You blessed me with! I'm so sorry! Please forgive me!"

James 5:16 says that the "fervent prayer of a righteous man avails much." Well, I wasn't exactly righteous, but I was certainly begging God fervently. I was praying like a man going to trial facing a life sentence. I pleaded with Him just as I had countless times before during a crisis, but there was something very different about this crisis situation. I wasn't just looking to live to see another day after an overdose, hoping He would heal my mom when she had cancer or my children when they each had suffered near tragic accidents as toddlers, or that my wife wouldn't walk out on me after one of our countless fights. No, something very different was going on within my soul on this night in 6 bravo 24.

It was so dark and cold within that cell, and I was so terrified. I honestly was only hoping God would somehow allow me to fall asleep so that I could wake up the next morning in the comfort of my own apartment with Teddy, only to discover it was just a terrible dream.

I began praying, no, meditating within my head, "Please take away my worries, my anxieties, and my fears! Please take away my worries, my anxieties, and my fears!" I kept repeating those words over and over to Him. I knew if I cried out to God, He would come. He always came when I needed Him, and I needed Him now more than any other time in my life.

Then, these words came to me out of nowhere. "Ye though I walk through the valley of the shadow of death, I shall fear no evil, for Thou art with me" (Ps. 23:4). Although, at the time, I had no idea where it came from or how it came to me, I would later hear Jesus say in John 14:26 that He would bring remembrance of all the things that He had said to me. Obviously, I had read Psalm 23 at some point in my pre-addiction life, and at the darkest point in my life, in the darkest of jail cells, my faithful old Friend kept His promise.

I hadn't been to church except for a handful of times over the previous twenty years and certainly never opened the Bible, which collected dust while resting on our coffee table to impress visitors, but there it was embedded in my heart. I meditated on it, saying it over and over in my head. This went on for quite a while. How long, I'm not sure, but I must have repeated that verse literally dozens of times until I fell into almost a trance.

I did fall asleep, and it may have been the best darn sleep I had had in years, and I did wake up the next morning as well. But rather than being in the luxury of my apartment with Teddy, I was still in a jail cell with Mike and the realization that what had happened was certainly no dream.

That morning, however, would turn out to be especially different than any other morning in my life, before or after. No, it wasn't because I had never gotten up at 5 a.m. to the delight of jailhouse grits and a cup of grindy decaf. On this morning, I was different, and I've been wondering ever since what actually happened to me in the wee hours of that night on 2/7/07. Something had changed dramatically within me.

I remember my wife once saying she had three kids to take care of, our sons and me. She didn't lie. It was almost as if when I took that first hit on Henry's bong that I became stuck as a teenager, and I didn't want to grow up. I liked being a kid, and addiction helped me to escape the fear of having to be a responsible adult. First Corinthians 13:11 says, "When I was a child, I spoke as a child, I understood as a child; but when I became a man, I put away childish things." On the morning of 2/7/07, the Man Himself Jesus Christ was now living in me, and it was time to finally become a man.

The Fraternity of Brotherhood

Before my arrest, I had a very prejudiced opinion about inmates; after all, I had never been one, and all I really knew had been formulated from the TV, news, or urban legends. I was certainly very condescending. I looked at them as losers, people who were just flat-out lazy and put no effort into living a productive life. What's the old saying, "You never really know someone until you've walked a mile in their shoes"? Whoever said that must have spent some time in the "pen," I believe.

I learned almost instantly that inmates are almost like a fraternity, a brotherhood. There was an "us against the world" philosophy that existed amongst them, and the longer I was in there, the more I understood the deeply rooted foundation of its source. Sure, there were disagreements, even an occasional fight, from time to time, but the concept that people get raped, even killed, on a regular basis could not have been further from the truth. Sure, there were the hustlers who tried to turn two racks (packs) of cookies into three, but for the most part, the men looked out for each other and supported each other, and although most would never admit it, stemming from their upbringing, they loved each other. Suffering loves company, right?

Jailhouse Lingo

There was a system of nicknames used to simplify and identify people. A man's name was only used if they didn't qualify for one of the common aka's. African Americans were labeled according to their color. The darker complexion men were called "Black." If you were mixed or had a lighter skin color, you were called "Red." Mexicans and anyone of Spanish decent were called "Chicos." Caucasians were termed "Crackers." Anyone with a bald head was referred to as "Bald head" or would have their name attached, such as "Bald Ed." If you were tall and thin, you were called "Slim." The teenage kids were "Jits," short for jitterbugs. The older, wiser inmates were called "Pops" or "OGs" (old-school gangster) as a term of endearment. Sometimes you were named after the state you came from. Although certainly a "Cracker," I was also taller than the majority and was promptly named "Big Dave."

The black inmates dubbed the recreation yard as "Cracker Beach" since that was the only area where the white guys could lay out in the sun to tan. Cracker Beach during the day and my bunk late at night were the two places where God's presence was the strongest within me. I could sit shirtless with my legs crossed in the sunlight, meditating on God's Word while working on my tan, and often near the middle of the basketball court, and nobody cared. We'd have a four-on-four basketball game going on with me sitting right there. I could feel God's shield around me. The ball never hit me. It was as if my brothers enjoyed protecting me. Anytime the ball got even remotely close, they would apologize to me. It's impossible to explain what that shield felt like, the feeling of the Holy Spirit's power.

I was housed with murderers, child molesters, and pretty much every other kind of criminal, and in no way did I ever feel in danger. In fact, I had never felt so free and so safe as I did sitting on that basketball court in my entire life.

Demon-Possessed

I had heard once that you know a person has become demon-possessed when they change from one type of person into someone who is completely different. Well, I certainly fit the mold. I was a dead man walking. I was on death row, just waiting for my number to be called, and the sooner, the better. I don't know what was hurting worse, the complete and utter mental, physical, or spiritual loneliness, or having to coexist in a completely lifeless body with the destroyer (Satan), who had bullied his way in and now had complete control over me. I had become so afraid of myself that I could barely lift my head to look into the mirror when, or if, I'd brush my teeth out of the shear fear of what I'd see.

I was undeniably demon-possessed. I could see tiny bugs crawling out of my cheeks, and I'd take needles and try digging them out. I'd dig deeper and deeper until my face was left bleeding and scarred. My eyes appeared to be completely black, almost snake-like. Hmm, snake-like, how completely appropriate.

I truly could not recognize myself; it filled me with even more fear, and fear is possibly the most common denominator amongst addicts.

Years later, on a Sunday morning at the beginning of a church service at my church, Crossover Church in Tampa, Pastor Tommy "Urban D" Kyllonen asked the question to our church, "Can a Christian have a demon?" He proceeded to answer, "No," then explained why. Once a person believes in his heart that Jesus Christ died on the cross for their sins and then rose from the grave on the third day, that person is then saved and receives the indwelling of the Holy Spirit, which takes up residence in the body of that person for all eternity (their body becomes the temple of the Holy Spirit (1 Cor. 6:19).

Jesus said, "He lives with you and will be with you" (John 14:17), and a demon cannot inhabit a house that Jesus resides in.

After service that Sunday morning on my drive home, I broke down crying. The truth of what Pastor T revealed hit me like a ton of bricks.

The first forty-six years of my life, I had always believed I was saved because I believed in God and prayed every night when the truth was that I had only received the prevenient grace that God sends out to all people (Titus 2:11), but I had not yet received the saving grace that only comes by accepting Christ as our Savior.

If I had died after my first overdose at eighteen years of age or after any of the other overdoses thereafter, I would have spent all eternity in outer darkness, in hell, completely separated from God forever.

I cried uncontrollably out of my deepest gratefulness to God for His grace and unimaginable love for me. He kept me alive all those years, patiently waiting for me to humbly receive Christ at just the perfect time to begin fulfilling the plan He had for my life.

A New Creation

When I got down off my bunk the morning of 2/7/07, I remember taking a deep breath and then exhaling. It was almost like I was inhaling a new life and blowing out the old one. I felt good, man! "What the heck is going on?" I thought. I'm in jail in an orange jumpsuit getting ready for the first of many breakfasts at "Cafe Orient Road," yet I felt good, relieved somehow, filled with a "peace that goes beyond understanding" (Phil. 4:6).

I remember standing in front of the shiny piece of tin in our cell that doubled as a mirror, and as I gazed into it, I could see my family sitting around a dinner table holding hands and praying before a meal, something we had never done. The picture filled me with unimaginable hope. We rarely ate together anymore, and we certainly never prayed together at the dinner table or anywhere else, for that matter. Was God showing me my future in that jail cell mirror? I wasn't really sure, but I do know that something deep within me was saying, "Everything is going to be okay." Romans 15:3 says, "May the God of hope fill you with all joy and peace in believing, that ye may abound in hope, through the power of the Holy Spirit."

I was filled with overwhelming hope. "My life is finally going to change," I told myself. I had a feeling of such great relief, as if a massive weight had been removed from my shoulders. I was locked within a jail, yet I felt freer than I ever had in my life, and although there remained the potential of a very long prison sentence, that pending sentence paled in comparison to being freed from the life sentence I had been serving within my mind. I was truly free for the first time since childhood, and I looked forward to going home in a couple of days and experiencing an exciting new life, no matter what it would entail.

Time for Court

The exhilaration of my born-again experience was short-lived, however. This was my second stay at the Orient Road facility. During the first trip, I was so petrified that I only left my cell when called at meals, and even then, sometimes I passed and remained within the safety and seclusion of my bunk. This time was completely different in every way. I was a seasoned "con," I suppose you could say.

I knew all the jailhouse routines and rituals, so feeling comfortable, I took a stroll outside to the recreation yard. The rec yard was basically an enclosed room with twenty-foot-high cinder block walls approximately fifty feet long and fifty feet wide. It had a basketball hoop, and the roof was open to allow us delinquents the luxury of viewing the sky.

As I leaned against the wall by myself watching the guys play ball, my eyes drifted up into the blue sky. Suddenly, I felt like my old self again; my newly acquired faith and hope balloon had quickly burst and was replaced with a head filled with worry and fear and anxiety. "What had I done?" The officer had told me that the charges were very serious. "How long would I be in here?" I thought. "Would I be getting out when I went to court in a couple of days?"

Within a couple of days, I was scheduled to start the drug program that I had been sentenced to for my November arrest, and I was excited to get my new life started, but what if? I began sweating, and my heart was beating like crazy as if during a panic attack. I quickly returned to my cell in an effort to locate that feeling of peace that had arisen the morning of 2/7/07.

I lay on my bunk and again began searching deep within my soul for that place where I had located it, that secret place where God is. I began begging Him for that peace again, "Please come back! Please come back!" And it did.

This anomaly seemed to occur nonstop for quite a few days, the feeling of indescribable peace, only to be interrupted within moments by the expected angst of a man on the verge of losing one of the few possessions that remained in his life: his freedom.

They hold the crazy husbands seventy-two hours before the joy of being brought before the king of the court for their impending judgment. I suppose it's to hopefully allow them to calm down a bit or perhaps sober up just in case they receive the privilege of being released back into the real world again.

They woke us up at 4:00 a.m. to eat real quick, then cuffed us and drove us downtown for court; 4:00 a.m. to get to court twenty minutes away, which didn't even open till 9:00 a.m.

I had been acquainted with handcuffs, but when they lead you chained together with a dozen or so fellow inmates with your feet shackled and tuck you into a pitch-dark paddy wagon for the before-dawn journey downtown to the courthouse, that is something that either turns you into a man or humbles you into feeling like a mass murderer. I suppose it did the latter to me.

It may sound a bit bizarre, but I was excited about the opportunity to display my newfound halo before my now ex-wife. Yes, it had only been three days since I was carted away from her driveway wearing shiny steel bracelets, but I was a miraculously changed man, and I was sure she'd see it and immediately notice the difference within me.

However, there would be no reunion of our souls in the middle of the courtroom floor on that morning. In fact, we wouldn't even be in the same room together. I was brought into a room filled with dozens of other anxiety-filled felony offenders dressed in their finest orange jumpsuits to sit in front of some sort of movie screen showing an empty court room. "What? This is court?" I thought.

We sat there for what seemed like an eternity until a movement finally appeared on the courtroom movie set, and as I watched, filled with disappointment, members of the court slowly entered one by one and took their rightful places to await the grand entrance of the all-powerful Oz. I scanned the room with great anticipation, searching for my ex, but the view was limited only to the judge's bench.

Then the announcement was made, "All rise for the honorable judge . . ." Huh? Rise for what? Could he even see us sitting here squirming in our seats? I didn't believe he could since not once during the proceedings did he ever look up. He merely focused on the documents in front of him for each case and quickly rendered his decisions. Nevertheless, we all stood as he entered the courtroom, took his seat, and then instructed us all to be seated. I continued to search the courtroom for even a glimpse of my ex, but still, nothing could be seen but the mean ogre who held my life in his hands.

Finally, my name was called. I stood, and they announced the charges. There were four counts of violating a domestic violence injunction, along with two counts of aggravated stalking, a total of six felonies. The judge then turned his head to the left and asked, "Are you afraid, ma'am?" And then the camera, almost in slow motion, rotated toward her, and I saw her, well, at least the top of her head anyway. His question was directed at my ex. Her head was bowed, and I couldn't hear her answer, but I clearly witnessed her head sobbingly nod up and down. I felt so terribly bad for her that I almost wished that I hadn't been able to see her at all that morning rather than have to share in her obvious pain.

The judge, almost instantly, as if he had already predetermined my fate, announced, "Bond denied. You may take him away." What? No bond? What did that mean? I was not going home?

Yes, I was excited at the prospect of unleashing the new David on my ex, but I was just as excited about the certainty of going home and starting my new life.

When I arrived back at the POD, I was questioned several times by the guys, "What are you doing back here? What happened?" All I could say was, "I don't know. The judge said, 'no bond.' He didn't even give me another court date." Some were suspicious that maybe I had done a little more than just have a disagreement with my ex-wife. They assumed there must have been some very serious violence involved for me not to have been released. After all, I had been given the drug program sentence for my November arrest, and I had no prior convictions on my record.

First-time offenders almost always get assigned a court date and then released on bond for time served. It was becoming very clear to me that something out of the norm was happening in my case. In fact, it was becoming crystal clear that everything surrounding my stay at Hotel Orient Road was becoming very peculiar, mysterious even.

Consumed by the Bible

A s I walked back to my cell, all I could think was, "I may be in here a while." Yet, even with that prospect, I wasn't especially worried. Something inside me assured me that the more time spent there, the better . . . very peculiar indeed.

Upon entering my cell to a lounging Mike, my eyes were immediately drawn like a magnet to steel to a brand new Gideon's New Testament pocket Bible that was resting comfortably on the steel shelf that substituted as a desk. I asked Mike if I could look at it, and he responded, "Go ahead, man . . . I don't look at it." I picked it up, climbed to my top bunk, and lay down comfortably, then began reading God's Word, or rather I was absorbing it. I had read it occasionally as a teen alone in the quiet of my parents' basement and distinctly remember feeling glimpses of the same peace and tranquility that I was now receiving, but this time, it was much different. When I first heard Jesus begin to speak in Matthew chapter 3, a whole new world slowly began opening up within me.

Romans 10:17 says, "Faith comes from hearing, and hearing by the word of God." I was not only reading His words, but I was also hearing them in my heart. I could see Him directly in front of me speaking to me, and I believed every single word He was saying. It was almost as if I was watching a movie about Him, and He was talking solely to me. I could see Him right in front of me as He gestured calmly with His hands as He spoke. There were no disciples around or deputies or convicts, for that matter; it was just me and Jesus, and His words were piercing my heart.

I became instantly captivated by Him. I absorbed every word of His as if my life depended on it, which, come to find out, it did. The peace His words gave me was overwhelming. My old Friend had renewed our relationship so quickly and so powerfully that I had to force myself to take occasional breaks.

When I did put the Bible down and try to do any normal jail activities, such as frequenting the rec yard, eating meals, or walking about the POD, I felt a noticeable loss of His peace. So, I would repeatedly return to my bunk and continue reading. Each time I repeated this sequence, the results were the same. His peace would return as I read and then would withdraw, or leave, when I stopped. It came and went very noticeably as I tried to comprehend its significance. I had no idea what was going on. All I knew was that I liked it and desperately needed it.

It was as if I was instantly filled with God's love and just as immediately began sharing that love with all the inmates and the deputies. I told everybody that I loved them—complete strangers. I remember approaching one of my favorite inmates, a dude named Sean "Red" Collier. I told him I loved him, and as I leaned forward to hug him, he backed away and said, "Oh no, no," and gave me a fist bump instead.

I would later learn that according to the National Center For Fathering eight-five percent of youths in prison come from fatherless homes. Most never had a relationship with their fathers. Many had dads who they had never even met, were incarcerated, or just did not want anything to do with them. It was understandable how men who basically had elementary school educations (in our POD, there were approximately seventy men, and only one other inmate and I had a high school diploma) had an upbringing that not only lacked discipline or parental guidance but also lacked any form of love.

The saying that "you never truly know someone until you've walked a mile in their shoes" began to take on a whole other meaning with me. I have said that everybody should have to spend a year in jail. It'll certainly change the way you look at the less fortunate and undoubtedly instill a new compassion for your fellow man; it sure did with me, anyway. I have never looked at the poor and needy and oppressed the same ever since.

Made D.J.
My Power of Attorney

A month after my transformation, I needed to figure out a way to continue paying child support to my ex. God requires us to pay our debts, and since I was still restricted from contacting her because of the restraining order, I gave D.J. power of attorney. I explained to him how to withdraw funds from my retirement account and advised him how much to give her and when.

Romans 12:2 says to "be transformed by the renewing of your mind." Christ had changed me completely, and although she was the one who had put me in jail, I also realized that it was God who kept me there to fulfill His purpose for me. I still had nothing but love for her and wanted to make sure I kept the support coming.

By God's grace, I had "put off the old man . . . and brought on the new one" (Eph. 4:22, 24), so much so that I also informed D.J. to get rid of all my stuff: furniture, clothes, everything. I was a brand new man and wanted to start completely over, and I'll be darned if he didn't; he only left me with a black pair of Air Jordans.

I was so committed to this transformation that I shaved off my beard and also began shaving my head bald. I was a completely new creation in Christ from the inside out.

It was interesting that I would read later in the Bible that Apostle Paul had also shaved his head after making a vow (Acts 18:18).

I Had Received the Holy Spirit

As the days proceeded, and I waited to be assigned a court date, all my awakened hours were spent reading my Bible. It became a permanent part of me. I carried it everywhere I went. I took it to meals with me, I toted it out in the rec yard, I carried it with me on walks around the POD, and I even slept with it in my hand. I knew that it was the source of my newfound peace and hope, and I was afraid to put it down and risk losing it.

As I continued to eat His words fifteen to twenty hours a day, the answer to the mystery that was happening within me was finally revealed. In John 16:7, Jesus instructed the disciples, saying, "It is to your advantage that I go away; for if I do not go away, the Helper will not come to you; but if I depart, I will send Him to you." I had just finished reading about the Helper, the Comforter, the Holy Spirit, in John 14, and my heart leaped for joy within me! He had sent me the Holy Spirit. No other person could possibly comprehend the importance of this revelation to me. I had finally found the "it" that I had been searching for my entire life.

I had cried out to God many times throughout my life, usually when I was terrified about a situation of various sorts, and He always came to my rescue . . . always. So, I just figured God was somewhere way out in the universe chilling on a cloud with angels feeding Him grapes, and if I yelled loud enough and cried hard enough, He'd hear me and feel sorry for me and come save me, which He always did, without fail. But at this moment—the single most important moment of my life—I realized that God wasn't just real, but He was also literally living within me. He wasn't just close by; He was within me, in front of me, behind me, and alongside me.

God is everywhere at all times. He literally fills the entire universe at the same time. Shoot . . . I realized that God is so big that the entire universe is within God. Wow! And this mighty God had now made a home within David Scott Gaskill. Life-changing doesn't even scratch the surface.

Jesus would go on to say in John 14:27, "Peace I leave to you, My peace I give to you; not as the world gives do I give to you." The pieces of the puzzle were perfectly coming together one scripture at a time. My whole adult life, I was searching for the peace that my soul had always been longing for, yet I was searching in all the wrong places, wrong people, and wrong things. Just as my lifetime best Friend said: His peace can't be found in the world or the things of the world. It can only be found in Jesus Christ.

Began Serving

"The lamp of the body is the eye. If therefore your eye is good, your whole body will be full of light. But if your eye is bad, your whole body will be full of darkness . . ." (Matt. 6:22–23).

The days proceeding 2/7/07 were as if a light switch had been turned on within my soul. I went from complete darkness to being filled with the light and the love of God, and I had no choice but to share that love with everyone. I was like "a man who found a treasure in a field and in my joy I was willing to sell that treasure and buy the whole field" (Matt. 13:44). I was all in and began loving and serving my fellow inmates in any way I possibly could. Just like "Jesus did not come to be served, but to serve" (Matt. 20:28), I began serving my brothers like a waiter at a restaurant. I would take all the chairs down off the dining tables for everybody in the POD and situate them to get ready to eat before each meal.

I took the scripture, "So the last will be first, and the first last," (Matt. 20:16) literally. I would always go to the back of the line when it was time to get our dog food just in case there weren't enough trays; I wanted to make sure everybody else got theirs, and I'd go without if necessary. When they were finished with their meals, I would go table to table like a busboy, gathering all the empty trays and carrying them to the kitchen to be washed. Then, I would wipe off the tables and put the chairs back on top of them when chow time was over.

We all had assigned chores to perform throughout the day, so I would look for the worst jobs to do, the ones no one else wanted, of which cleaning the bathroom was at the top of the list. It was so saddening to realize that the men were actually children in men's bodies.

Most had the mentality of a juvenile and acted as such. They would urinate on the floor. They'd wipe their behinds and toss the toilet paper on the floor; it was almost like an act of rebellion against the establishment, which amused them to no end. When I'd enter the bathroom, it was if a feces bomb had been set off, but it did not bother me one bit. I enjoyed serving my brothers. Anything that I could do to make a terrible situation for the world's less fortunate a little better, I was more than willing to do so.

I received money each month from my brother and his wife and my parents to purchase canteen (snacks such as chips, cookies, and candy, as well as hygiene products). When the canteen carts would arrive in the POD every two weeks, I can remember the horrible looks on the faces of the poorest of inmates who didn't receive anything while I was always getting a big sack of goods. I felt selfish, even greedy, so I began seeking out all my brothers who were indigent (indigent meant they had no money and only received two free envelopes and two stamps) and began taking orders for each of them. I made sure that everyone in the POD got at least a rack of cookies or a candy bar before I ordered anything for myself. Seeing how just a small gesture like that dramatically changed their continence gave me more joy than any Snickers ever could, and I immediately began understanding the truth in Jesus's statement "that it is more blessed to give than to receive" (Acts 20:35).

The Doc Comes with My Meds

Approximately two weeks after my arrival, the jail doctor summoned me to his office to administer my anti-depressants, and psych medications, as well as a few other goodies. When you go through booking, you have to fill out a form listing all your medications and ailments. But that was on 2/6/07; that was before the miracle of 2/7/07.

I looked the doc in the eye and said, "Doc, I don't need any of those meds, sir."

He said, "Oh yes, you do . . . you got a lot of things going on."

I told him, "You don't understand, sir. I've never felt better in my life!" I'll never forget his look.

"Why are you so happy?"

"That's what I'm trying to tell you . . . something happened to me!"

He promised he'd come back with my meds when I changed my mind. By the grace of God, I've never had to take those meds ever since.

Met Jean Duncombe

A few days after the judge sent me back to my cell in limbo, I received an unexpected visit from a defense attorney named Jean Duncombe (who is a good friend of mine to this day). She said that a friend of mine named Biggy had sent her to help me arrange for a bond hearing. Good ole Biggy, always looking out for his golden goose. Judging later by the threatening letters he would send to me in jail, he was only interested in one thing, and it wasn't my freedom. He knew that as long as I was behind bars, his gravy train would be derailed. Jean advised me that she could arrange for the hearing rather quickly (within thirty days) and was very optimistic, considering I had no prior history of violence, that I'd receive bond and be released pending a court date. Although I was more than ready to go home, I was content to patiently wait a couple more weeks to start my new life. I had also been advised by one of the deputies that Teddy would be held safely in the dog pound until the outcome of the bond hearing, which also added to my well-being.

My Sons' Visits

While staying at Orient Road and Falkenburg jails, I would fill out the visitor form for the same time for my kids to visit every day, and I wrote to them to let them know the time. Every day, I'd sit and pray while anxiously waiting for my beloved sons to show up.

It was a month before I received a visit, and it was only my oldest son. He sat on one side of the glass window that separates the inmates from visitors, and I sat on the other side dressed in my bright orange jumpsuit. I can't even imagine what he must have felt seeing his dad, the inmate, for the first time. He informed me that Adam just wasn't ready to see me. I was filled with the excitement of the new me, and I couldn't wait to tell David all about Jesus. What had happened to me was so exciting and so powerful that I couldn't keep it to myself. I had to tell everyone what God had done for me, especially my family.

I was preaching hard to my son during that first visit when he interrupted me. His voice was filled with disappointment and sadness when he said, "You like it in there, don't you?"

I quickly assured him, "Oh no, son. I would much rather be out there with you, but something really amazing has happened to me."

It was another month before I'd see him again. I remember the deputy announcing over the loud speaker, "Gaskill, you have a visitor." I told him that it must be a mistake because I had forgotten to fill out the form for that particular day.

Then, the kind deputy informed me that someone else's visit canceled, so he allowed me the visit. I had no clue who it could be, but much to my astonishment, it was D.J., and this time, Adam was with him. I was so excited and had tears of joy! I was jumping up and down, yelling to the inmates, "My son is here! My son is here!" Both of my boys were laughing as I walked to my seat in front of the glass.

However, as I took my seat, the smiles disappeared into the sadness of seeing their once hero behind a glass wall. Adam was sobbing with his head down as D.J. put his arm around him. All I could say was, "Don't cry, son . . . everything is gonna be alright. This is the best thing that could have happened to me. If I had gotten out in three days, I'd be dead by now. This had to happen."

As a first-time offender, I should have been released from jail after three days. At that point, I was realizing that nothing happening to me was normal. I could feel that there was something divine going on and sensed that God had other plans up His sleeve for me. "What the devil had intended for evil God had intended for my good" (Gen. 50:20) and the good of my family.

They didn't visit much after that (maybe three or four times), and when they did, they were always in a hurry to get outta there and cut the hour-long visits short. I remember a lifetime criminal tell me that he never let his kids visit cause he didn't want them to see him in there. It wasn't until later that I began to understand his rationale. The excitement of seeing my sons was always short-lived as soon as they'd leave and I'd return to my empty cell (I was blessed with my own cell after a month at Orient), and I'd get on my knees and cry my heart out to God; the pain of not being able to hug and hold them was, by far, the hardest part about being incarcerated. However, I continued to write them several times a week, preaching hard; that seemed to be all I could do anymore.

Officer Evil

The inmate diet was supposed to consist of 2000–2200 calories a day, which is a starvation diet to most people, and we indeed were all starving. It was interesting how stupid they think we all were, or maybe they just didn't care. I only had to be there a few days to realize that Chicken Royale, Chicken Tetrazzini, and Chicken Scampi were all the same, just with different names and something poured on top to give it a different appearance.

I later would calculate the calories for every single item they fed us, and except for the four slices of bread each day, our diets totaled more like 1400 calories. After a couple of months of daily exercise (there wasn't much else to do in there) and being deprived my lifelong pizza and fast food intake, I had my first six-pack abs since being a high schooler. If it weren't for the canteen supplements, I would have shriveled up and blown away.

In 6 Bravo, we had a deputy who was nicknamed Officer E. E was for Estavez but more appropriately could have stood for Officer Evil. E was not a very nice man, to say the least. Most of the deputies were pretty cool; however, there's a bad apple in every bushel, and E was that bad apple. He liked to antagonize us by taking the extra trays of food at the end of each meal and slowly scraped the food off into a trash can right in front of us while laughing at us as we looked on in horror.

I prayed to God what to do, and He was clear. After all, it was no accident that He had strategically placed me amongst hundreds of homeless and poor and needy and uneducated men. Shoot, I should have served three days in jail and been released to go my merry way, but that wasn't God's plan, and I knew in my spirit that He had a greater purpose for me. He commanded me, "Speak up for the people who have no voice, for the rights of all the misfits. Speak out for justice! Stand up for the poor and destitute" (Prov. 31:8–9 MSG).

The next day, I approached Officer E at his desk and asked for permission to chat for a minute, and he said fine. I explained to him that all the inmates were extremely hungry, and since there were always several extra trays after each meal, would it be possible that he put the extra trays on the tables for the inmates to share rather than throw them out? To my utter astonishment, he agreed and gave us the extra food.

Obviously, the inmates were thrilled, but there was one more thing I could do for them. We were served what we nicknamed "Jim Jones juice" with our meals. The nickname came from the theory that they were trying to kill us with that stuff. It was a sugar-free juice served at each meal, and although it was nothing special, it was better than nothing. After we received our trays, we would approach the cooler to fill up our coffee cup with Jim Jones. Most of the deputies would let us get seconds, but not Officer E. He'd give us one cup, and then he would pour out the whole cooler into the sink. So I prayed again, and again, God instructed me.

Joshua 1:9 was and is one of my all-time favorites, "Have I not commanded you? Be strong and of good courage, do not be afraid, nor be dismayed, for the Lord your God is with you wherever you go." So, I was filled with courage as I approached E at his desk once again. This time, I employed a different tactic to gain his favor. I wrote him a note and thanked him for giving us the extra trays and informed him that God had asked me to ask him to allow the inmates to have the extra juice as well rather than throw it out. He just kinda laughed but didn't respond.

That night, one of my best friends, who was a trustee, pulled me aside and was very upset. "Man, you shouldn't have said anything to that dude! Dag, man, why couldn't you just leave him alone!"

"What's wrong?" I asked.

"You shouldn't have said anything about the juice."

I told him I was trying to help the inmates and there was nothing wrong with that.

Sent to Psych Ward

The next morning, E was off duty, but I got summoned to the desk, and the deputy took me into a back office where two guys in white coats were waiting to interrogate me.

"Are you hearing voices?"

I quickly replied, "Well, yes, God is talking to me." I mean, what was I supposed to say? I wasn't gonna lie to them. That was all they asked and left as I was sent back to my cell.

The next morning, the deputy instructed me to pack up my stuff; I was being transferred. It wasn't unusual for inmates to get moved, but this was my first time, and I was comfortable in 6 Bravo and had several good friends there. As they escorted me out, I remember the look of sadness on the face of the inmate who told me I shouldn't have said anything to E.

I asked where they were taking me, but got no response as they led me outside to a paddy wagon. They were transporting me from Orient Road Jail to Falkenburg Jail. When we got to Falkenburg, I knew something wasn't right as we walked toward the psych ward. Wow! They were putting me in lockdown with all the other crazy people who were hearing voices!

The psych ward was bad . . . real bad. The cells were filthy! There was urine and feces on the walls. There were bugs everywhere, and you slept on a concrete slab. There was a slot in the door where they slid in your tray of food, and you got five minutes to eat, or they took it away. You were only allowed out of the cell for an hour a day to walk around or shower, although they weren't too concerned about adhering to those rules.

I went a couple of days without ever getting out, and they didn't give me any toilet paper the first few days I was in lockdown. I wasn't permitted to make any phone calls, and there was no canteen in there.

Before getting there, I was writing to my sons several times a week. I was excited about my new life with God and wanted to make sure I documented everything. However, when I was locked down, they didn't permit me to have paper or a pencil. I remember sitting on my bunk and laughing with joy as I knew Satan was trying to shut me up. I had no fears . . . I had no worries . . . God was with me wherever I went.

When I first arrived, there was a lot of screaming and hollering going on. One inmate was pounding on his cell door and yelling, "All night long. All night long." I was pretty sure he wasn't singing the Lionel Richie song, although I wish he was, but rather, he was yelling and banging all night long. I thought he'd never stop as I prayed to God that he would so I could sleep.

The Angel in
the Psych Ward

That night, I had my first angel sighting in jail. "Do not forget to entertain strangers, for by so doing some have unwittingly entertained angels" (Heb. 13:2). This stranger was certainly an angel, yet he was the one entertaining me.

As I lay on my bunk late at night, I looked up and noticed someone standing outside my door, staring at me through the small glass panel. It was very unusual since no one was allowed outside of their cells at night in lockdown, but even so, I wasn't alarmed one bit. Then, I realized it was the man who had been pounding on his cell door and yelling, "All night long." He was completely normal, very peaceful, and calm. I got up and stood a foot away from him on my side of the glass, and he smiled and said, "You look like a movie star." I smiled a huge smile, and then we proceeded to have the most pleasant and amazing conversation as I listened to him, completely mesmerized as to what was occurring. He began talking about several different places I had recently visited before relocating to Florida, places I hadn't discussed with any of the inmates, let alone this complete stranger. It was as if he knew everything about me and was certainly another of the many miracles the good Lord would manifest to me during my time in jail.

Another Angel in the Psych Ward

After a couple of nights in my new crib, I noticed a dirt smudge that was about five to six feet up on the wall. When all the lights in the ward went out except the night lights, the smudge came to life. There is no other way to explain it. It transformed into a face that came out of the wall. I eventually sketched this person a couple of times when a nice guard gave me some paper and a rubber pencil (crazy people weren't allowed real pencils, and I still have the sketches). I can only believe He was an angel of the Lord. Although I couldn't see Him talking, we were conversing through our thoughts, and He gave me great peace and comfort as I'd sit there and talk with Him until I fell asleep each night.

The Doctor's Visit

I finally received a visit from the psychiatrist a few days after my arrival in lockdown. He talked to me for about five minutes, then said, "Why are you in here? There's nothing wrong with you." I completely agreed, and he said he'd get me discharged the next day.

Six days went by before they came to transfer me. However, they didn't send me back to the main population; they sent me back to the Orient Road Jail psych ward instead. After another six days in paradise and a festive Easter dinner, I was finally released back to the main population.

When the time came, I requested to go back to my original pod, 6 Bravo, and the deputy looked at me like I really was crazy. He asked why I'd want to go back there . . . Officer E was still there, and I informed him that I had a lot of friends there, and besides, I wanted Officer E to see that I forgave him. The deputy didn't agree with my request but gave in to my wishes, and they proceeded to transfer me back to Orient Road Jail.

When I arrived in 6 Bravo, Officer E was sitting at his desk, and as I walked right up to him, he looked like he had seen a ghost, or possibly he had a revelation, and it was the Holy Ghost he saw. I smiled softly and said hello, then went to my new cell upstairs, 6B48, a one-man cell, which I loved because of the privacy. I'll never forget that when I put my belongings away and then, before taking a seat at my new desk, I looked down to see that the words "Big Dave" were carved into the wooden chair. All I could do was smile, and I'm sure it was one heck of a smile as, once again, God manifested Himself to me and continued to show me He was with me wherever I went.

God Wrote Me a Poem

It was in that cell in 6 Bravo, the first pod I was in during my stay in jail and the place where I received salvation in Christ when God spoke through me once again. However, this time, I was completely alone in the quiet and privacy of my own cell when I witnessed another powerful occurrence of the Holy Spirit. As I was moved, I grabbed a pad of paper and a pencil, sat down at my desk, and wrote the following poem in just a matter of minutes. Although I had a gift for writing poetry, even before Christ changed me, this was different. It was basically my life and testimony, all wrapped up in this beautiful poem or psalm, if you will. It flowed perfectly, and I barely had to think or change anything, which is why I knew it was written by God and for His glory.

The Night My Life Changed Forever

When darkness was all around me,
When I thought there was no solution,
When "the dog" had his grips on me,
There was but one resolution.

I could think of no way out
Of the darkness of the "pits of Hell."
Everything was lost, and everybody was gone,
And the aroma of death was all I smelled.

The time had come to finally end it.
There was just nothing else to do.
The devil had finally conquered me,
Till I came crying out to You.

"The Lord is my shepherd,
Please take away my worries, my anxieties, and my fears."
I repeated these prayers over and over to You
Till there was nothing left but tears.

I don't know if I even slept that night,
But this, I know for sure.
The pain and suffering had disappeared,
And the fear was there no more.

A peace had come upon me
In 6 Bravo 24.
The Spirit of Christ had saved me
When I came knocking upon His door.

What can I say about my Lord,
Except that God is good.
He changed my life, He saved me,
Like His promises said He would.

Now I cry out daily
Out of joy and love of life,
Amazed at His healing power,
Of His strength and of His might.

It's an amazing, incredible, and wonderful God
That all us Christians serve.
He died on the cross to save us,
A death He didn't deserve.

So when your days get dark and gloomy,
And you feel there's just no way.
Remember His amazing love for you,
And get on your knees and pray.

Seek Him with all your heart and soul,
And Christ Jesus, you will find.
He's there for each and every one,
To guard our hearts and minds.

I just want to thank You, Lord,
And praise Your glorious name!
For saving me in that cold dark cell,
Things will never be the same.
Amen.

I knew it was written by the Holy Spirit because it just flowed together instantly and perfectly.

Shortly after that, Officer E got demoted because of too many inmate complaints. God protects His children.

It's important to note that when inmates arrive at Orient Road Jail, they are there a couple of days and are either released or sent to Falkenburg Jail to await sentencing. It's unusual for an inmate to be housed in more than a couple of pods during their stay; however, God had me transferred from Orient to Falkenburg, back to Orient, and then back to Falkenburg once again.

I stayed in fifteen different pods, had twenty-one different cells/bunks during my incarceration, and I completely understand how and why the good Lord was using me. There were only sixty-nine other inmates in my original pod, 6 Bravo. However, by meticulously moving me around to different pods, I was able to witness to well over 1000 of this world's brokenhearted.

In each pod, I gave my testimony, held Bible studies, and started nightly prayer circles in the rec yards. I witnessed several of my brothers receive Christ.

Wilson Tells Me to Have Church

One night, while in the laundry room, I was folding the pod's laundry (a chore I actually enjoyed very much) when an inmate named Wilson approached me. "Big Dave, you're a preacher."

I laughed and told him, "No I'm no preacher . . . I'm a ball player." He then pleaded with me to have church services for the inmates. It was less than a month since I had committed my life to God, and I had only been reading the Bible for a few weeks, but God was working in me, and the inmates saw it even more than myself.

In my mind, I was thinking how I had been disobedient to God's calling my entire life, yet He never gave up on me and showed up for me on the worst night of my life. I had made a commitment in my heart that night, and I wasn't about to turn my back on Him now. To be honest, I was afraid of what the consequences would be if I did.

The next day, I went to the deputy who was on duty and told him that the inmates wanted me to have church services. I'll never forget his reaction.

"Church services! We don't have church in here." Then, it happened . . . he relented and said, "If you wanna have church services, you can do it out in the rec yard, but you can't do it in here." I was so excited and thanked him.

That night after dinner, Wilson and I walked around the pod and informed everyone that we were going to be having a church service outside at sundown. Wilson then helped me carry chairs out, and we set them up in rows of ten. It was such an amazingly beautiful sunset service. The yard was filled.

I started with prayer, and Wilson improvised a beautiful old black gospel song acapella, and he literally sounded like an angel. I was in such awe at what God was doing through us. Many of us had tears coming down our cheeks as I began preaching on Psalm 23, "Ye though I walk through the valley of the shadow of death . . .," the scripture that had saved my soul on that cold dark evening of 2/7/07.

At the end of the service, we all got together in a big circle, held hands, and prayed together. That night was the start of many beautiful sunset services and prayer circles, and I was given the honorable title of "Preacherman."

The Public Defender's Offer

It was March 2007 when I was blessed with my first experience with a public defender and learned quickly why they are referred to as "public pretenders." I remember talking to mine for the first time. He never once visited me in jail; he just called and informed me that they were offering me three years in prison and then acted like I should be grateful since six felonies could warrant seven years if I went to trial.

I remember yelling at him, "What, are you freaking kidding me! Three years for having a temper tantrum! I never touched her! I didn't even get near her! Forget it. I'll go to court!" Then, I promptly slammed the phone down.

As it turned out, Jean's offer to get me out in thirty days now looked pretty enticing, but I kept my promise to God to trust His plan. I also realized that I might be in there for quite a while.

On 4/25/07, a jury trial was scheduled for 7/23/07.

Chaplain with One Tooth

A lot of amazing things were happening to me in jail. God was showing Himself to me in so many powerful ways, not the least of which was a visit from a jail chaplain. He was a heavyset black man with one tooth. He asked me what the book was in my hand, and I told him it was the Alcoholic Anonymous blue book (I was attending meetings in jail).

He sternly said, "All the answers to life's problems are right here (showing me his well-worn Bible)." He was right. AA and NA (Narcotics Anonymous) have their purpose, but it is generally to help people stay sober, which is great, but it's only a start, a stepping stone.

The 12 Steps: 1.) Admit your powerless over drugs and alcohol. 2.) Believe in a power greater than yourself. 3.) Make a decision to turn your life over to God . . . and so on, are all spiritual principles and good ones; however, the organizations try to convince an addict that they have a disease, and if they practice these steps, they can become recovering addicts and will always be recovering from their disease. In other words, "once a pickle, always a pickle," I heard an old "dry drunk" say in a meeting.

No, no, no! That's a cop-out. Proverbs 23:7 says, "As a man speaks in his heart, so is he."

By God's grace, after the miracle of 2/7/07, I wasn't a pickle any longer.

I was an addict/alcoholic for twenty-eight years. I drank until I blacked out to escape the reality of any type of pain, hurt, or fear I was experiencing at that moment. But when it came to marijuana, cocaine/crack, and narcotic pain medications, I took them because I enjoyed the euphoria they provided, not because of any illness or disease and certainly not because I thought they'd fulfill the thirst my soul yearned for. I was searching for something, and although I was certainly sick spiritually, diabetes and cancer are diseases. Addiction and alcoholism are choices, in my humble opinion.

Shoot, I loved getting high, so much so that over the course of a couple of decades, I became so numb that I shamefully enjoyed it more than my own family.

AA and NA put the onus on the addict that they have to "work the steps" to be sober. It reminds me of the legalism of the Old Testament laws. The people thought that as long as they obeyed the law, they could get to heaven, but they didn't understand that the laws were meant to be spiritual (Rom. 7:14), and all that God ever wanted was their hearts.

When Christ died on the cross, it set us free from the bondage of the law (Col. 2:14). The soul of an addict, and everyone else for that matter, is searching for satisfaction and fulfillment, which can only be found by believing in Jesus from your heart.

My soul wasn't looking to be sober or recover. My soul was looking to be healed and set free from the bondage of addiction, and I didn't need to take twelve steps to achieve that freedom. I only had to take one, and that was believing in my heart that Jesus was my Lord God and Savior. It was by believing that in my heart that set my soul free. And by believing that and receiving His Holy Spirit, I received the power I needed to conquer all my weaknesses (Acts 1:8).

There's no point in being sober if you die and go to hell. All our souls want salvation. They want to be with God, be like God, and be with God for all eternity.

With my head down, I told the chaplain that I was facing a lot of time, and that set him on fire! He started quoting scripture after scripture and then asked me to turn to Luke 1:37 and read it out loud. So I did: "For with God, nothing will be impossible." The hairs on my arms are standing straight up as I remember his words.

"I've seen God erase records in the computer. I've seen Him drop charges. There ain't nothing God can't do!"

I don't remember anything else he said, but I definitely never read the blue book again and left that visit floating on air filled with the Spirit and hope.

When I returned to the pod, I immediately began boasting to the other inmates, "They are gonna drop the charges! They're gonna drop the charges! I know it." I distinctly remember another inmate reminding me that they had a record of all my phone calls and, "They got you, bro."

I knew what I knew in my heart. They were gonna drop the charges.

Second Meeting
with Jean

After agreeing with Ms. Duncombe at our initial meeting to proceed with filing for a bond hearing, I had an epiphany while deep in prayer one night. I had blown almost all my retirement fund on prodigious living and had only roughly $20,000 left, and I made the decision that what I had left would go to my ex-wife and my sons. I was willing to exercise my newfound faith in God and go with a public defender and accept whatever God's plan was for my life.

I called Ms. Duncombe to meet once again and informed her, with tears flowing down my face, that I wouldn't be needing her services and explained why. She was more than understanding, and even though I wasn't hiring her, she always made it a point to stop by and visit me whenever she was at the jail, a kind gesture that I'll never forget.

Roberto

was quickly promoted to a trustee position, along with a Mexican named Roberto Sanchez. Roberto was an illegal immigrant who had been charged with an armed robbery of a liquor store and was in Orient Road Jail awaiting a court date to most likely be extradited to Mexico.

Although mostly out of mere fear, many inmates run to God or anything else that they believe could save them. Roberto, however, was different. He caught my eye when I noticed him often surrounded by several other Mexican inmates. When I inquired what the Mexican gatherings were about, I was pleasantly informed that Roberto was also having Bible studies and prayer circles of his own. It certainly appeared that Roberto had had a conversion similar to my own.

It was late one very peaceful evening after lights out that I decided to take advantage of one of my trustee privileges (they left the trustees' cell doors open at night) and wandered downstairs to heat up some cookies and have some quiet time with the Lord in the common area; it was there that I came across Roberto already sitting there alone, reading his Bible.

Although he couldn't speak any English, and I couldn't speak a lick of Spanish, the most amazing thing happened that night.

As we sat next to each other, he pointed out to me the scriptures he was studying (his Bible was a Spanish version), and I was able to identify the book, chapter, and verses, and we began communicating. I don't know how to describe it; it was nothing less than a miracle. Although we were speaking different languages, God was interpreting to each of us what the other was saying through our thoughts.

Scripturally speaking, the only thing I can think of that even remotely resembled what happened that evening was the Pentecost (Acts chapter 2), when the Holy Spirit came over the disciples, and they began speaking in several different languages not their own to an audience of people from thirteen different countries, and they completely understood them.

I know I wasn't speaking Spanish in the wee hours of that night in 6 Bravo, and I know Roberto was not speaking English, but I distinctly remember the feeling of power and indescribable peace that came over me and my Mexican brother as I knew exactly what he was saying, and he understood exactly what I was saying as we bounced from passage to passage in joyful bliss for hours.

Those late-night Bible studies with my Mexican friend became a nightly ritual as Roberto became my best friend in the pod (we even remained pen pals for a couple of years after my release until he was deported to Mexico, and we lost touch).

He taught me my first Spanish sentences, and to this day, they are the two sentences that I use anytime I come across a Spanish person who can't speak English. "Jesus te ama" (Jesus loves you), and "Dios te bendiga" (God bless you).

When I was later transferred to a pod at Falkenburg Jail, while I was getting situated there for the first time, I was making my bunk and lifted the pad that serves as a mattress to tuck in my sheet, and God showed Himself once again. Written in black marker on the steel bunk were the words "Jesus te ama."

What Happened to Me the Night of 2/7/07

It took me several years to understand why my life changed so radically the night of 2/7/07. Overdose after overdose, I'd beg God to let me live and made empty promises that I'd stop the insanity if He did, and time after time, He'd let me live to see another day, and then when He did, I'd run right back to the dope man for another round.

God knows all of our thoughts before we even think them, and He certainly can see into our hearts and knows when we're lying and when we are sincere.

Throughout all my twenty-eight years of living in hell, He knew my promises were all just lies except for that night in that cold, dark cage. On that night, He knew I truly had had enough of being a junky and sincerely wanted to change. In my heart, I was sincerely humbled and finally ready to do things His way.

James 4:6 says, "God resists the proud but gives grace to the humble." Up until that night, I had been proud my entire life and always felt that I could stop the craziness whenever I desired. I remember thinking as soon as my first son was born that I'd stop and be the dad and godly example I was always meant to be. And then D. J. was born, and I spent that night celebrating at Buzz's Tavern, chugging liquor and snorting coke. Then, I promised on New Year's Day that would be my resolution and lied again and partied even harder. Then, I decided when Adam was born, that was finally gonna be it; I would change my life. Adam was born, and the madness continued on without interruption.

I promised and lied to God over and over for twenty-eight dreadful years until I had finally exhausted God's patience (if that's even possible), and out of His amazing love for me, He allowed me to be backed up against a cold jail cell cinder block wall with nowhere to run except to my ever-merciful Master. That was the moment when I finally lost my pride and begged for His help once again, only I was crying out of a pure heart and was truly ready to completely submit to His will and start doing things His way.

Psalm 30:5 says, "His anger is but for a moment, His favor is for life. Weeping may endure for a night, but joy comes in the morning." Now, if that scripture doesn't perfectly sum up the events of 2/7/07, I don't know what does.

Fast and Pump Removal

After being transferred to Falkenburg Jail, it was in one of those pods that I met a young man who we called Black Ed. On one occasion, when Jean Duncombe came to visit me, Ed noticed her when she was leaving and came over to me to inform me that she was his attorney. We got to talking and instantly became good friends. He was a Christian, and we took turns praying with the inmates.

One day, Ed sat at my table and gave me his tray. I thought he was just being friendly or possibly just wasn't feeling the meal of the day. When he told me he was fasting, I became curious. I had only been reading the Bible for three to four months and heard about fasting but didn't really know what it was about. Ed explained that it was a way of starving our flesh to feed our spirit. In other words, it was a way to draw closer to God, and I was all about that.

Not long after that, I decided to fast from food for a day.

That night in my cell, I had a weird bump appear on my lower back that was itching like crazy. As I scratched it, I felt something very abnormal. I lifted my shirt up and looked in the mirror, and to my shock, or amazement, I should say, there was a plastic tube the size of a coffee stirrer protruding from my back. I recognized that it was the catheter from the morphine pump. I immediately buzzed the deputy, who came promptly to my cell. I showed him my dilemma.

The deputies knew about my morphine pump because the jail had a specialist come in each month to fill it. I informed the deputy of the seriousness of my condition. If the pump ran out of morphine, it could stop working, and there was a chance it could explode within me, which could possibly be even fatal. There were good deputies and some not so good. Praise God, He sent me a good one who immediately rushed me to Tampa General in the middle of the night.

Once at the hospital, the doctors scurried around to find a specialist, which, in the middle of the night, was no easy task.

In the meantime, I was in a room handcuffed to my bed under arm guard like I was Hannibal Lecter. They kept me monitored the whole time as we waited for a pump specialist.

I had no fear, although it was very surreal to be outside the jail facility and in the real world for the first time in months. I had complete peace, but it was hard because, from my hospital room, I had a view of Harbour Island, where my family lived. They were so close yet so far away. I just wanted to call them so badly to let them know where I was but was prohibited. They did, after the fact, contact them just to let them know I was okay.

When the doctor finally arrived, he explained the procedure. He said they would have to cut me open to install a new catheter. I immediately told him no. I insisted that they remove the pump altogether. I told him I was fasting and that it was a sign from God that the pump should be removed for two reasons. I knew I was healed from my back pain and no longer needed it, and I also wanted to be completely drug-free for the first time in nearly three decades. They granted me my wish and removed the pump that night. In the morning, they ushered me back to Falkenburg's infirmary.

That first day, I was in such excruciating pain, and the devil was trying to convince me I had made a big mistake. "See, dummy, you need that pump. You need narcotics." I caved in and asked doctors for some pain medication, and they laughed at me. Seriously! I was lying there with a six-inch gash and staples on my side, and no pain meds? Well, nobody ever said jail was to be pleasant. But God was so good to me; the pain was quickly gone, and I was up and about in no time.

However, God had a plan. I was the only patient in the infirmary who wasn't bedridden. Those poor men. There were guys dying from cancer, AIDs, liver failure, and several who were paralyzed.

To be in jail is bad enough, but to be left to die in jail is unconscionable. I was filled with compassion for them. Since I was allowed to move about, I went from bed to bed, sat down next to each man, ministered to them, and prayed with them one-on-one. God had provided me with firsthand chaplaincy training to the highest degree. I loved those guys, and they loved me.

As I mentioned, there were good deps and bad deps; well, the infirmary was no exception.

Hippo

The patients in the infirmary were probably the most broken people that you could ever imagine. Only the sickest of all inmates stayed in the infirmary. Several had to be quarantined. To be so sick and also be locked up . . . well, it doesn't get much worse than that.

There was a trustee there named J.J. who served the food. J.J. was a very selfish, greedy, and insensitive young man. There was always extra food after meals, and a good trustee would share it amongst the inmates, but not J.J. He would hoard it and then sell it to the patients, usually for phone cards (a twelve-dollar card for five delicious meals). It was pretty hard to watch as he would take the cards from those who were so sick and hungry for food that he received for free.

One day, a diabetic patient was suffering from low blood sugar. He was sweating profusely and on the verge of passing out. I was running around the pod, trying to find something sweet for him to bring up his blood sugar. Unfortunately, canteen (snacks) was not allowed in the infirmary because of all the diabetics, but J.J. had a pitcher of juice, and that was just what the guy needed to bring up his blood sugar. I asked J.J. for it, and he said, "I'm not giving up my juice for that faker!"

I pleaded, "How could you be so selfish? It's only juice, and it could prevent him from going into a diabetic coma. Can't you, for once, put someone else before yourself?"

I remember J.J. saying, "No one puts anyone before themselves. Everyone looks out for number one!"

I told him that God said, "No one is to seek his own, but each one the other's well-being" (1 Cor. 10:24). "I would give my life for you!"

J.J. said, "You're a fake. He never put any food on my table, and no one puts anyone before themselves!"

There was a deputy in the infirmary named Mr. Smith. He wasn't very nice. He would always enter the pod, yelling and screaming at the patients who were already suffering enough. He was one of the few deputies who, I honestly could say, abused the inmates mentally and physically. They basically hated him.

One day when he arrived on duty, he was more pissed off than usual. He made an announcement: "Whoever wrote those curse words about me on the bathroom wall, stand up and have the guts to admit it. Be a man, you coward (talk about calling the kettle black)! If no one takes the blame for it, the whole pod will be locked down for the afternoon! On your beds, no TV, nothing!"

I got up quickly from my bed and walked toward the deputy. The pod was silent. Mr. Smith said, "Are you the one who did it, and are you going to take the punishment? You'll be put in the holding cell for thirty days and IDC'd (Inner Disciplinary Committee)!"

Obviously, the holding cell is not a very pleasant place to be, and being IDC'd meant additional time to your sentence. Knowing that "Blessed are those who are persecuted for righteousness sake" (Matt. 5:10), I said, "I'll take the punishment."

The deputy told me to go stand against the wall. I guess that was a way to humiliate me in front of the whole pod. I walked slowly over to the wall and stood there proudly and humbly with my head held high. The inmates loved me and were begging me, "Don't do it; you didn't write those words."

A nurse walked up to me and whispered, "Did you do it?" I told her quietly no. She asked, "Why are you gonna take the fall then?"

And I answered her, "To teach everyone an important lesson."

Mr. Smith came over, ranting and raving, and yelled at me to get in the cell, and after I did, he slammed the cold steel door shut!

The next day, the IDC officer came to visit me as part of the investigation. He began by saying, "Mr. Smith's report says you admitted to doing the crime and that you would do the punishment."

I quickly corrected him, "I said only that I would do the punishment." The officer asked, "Did you write those words?" I said that I had not. The officer also asked me why I was taking the punishment. I said, "I've been preaching to the inmates the importance of always putting others before themselves (Matt. 20:16). I must set the example for them. Please correct the report to read that I only said I would accept the punishment." He agreed that he would.

A few moments later, Mr. Smith entered the holding cell. He had a strange look on his face. He asked me, "Why did you accept the blame for something you didn't do?"

I repeated, "I'm trying to teach them to put others before themselves."

Smith looked at me and said, "I have to respect you for that."

At dinner that night, when J.J. came into the holding cell to give me my tray, I looked him softly in the eye and said, "See J.J., now do you believe that I would put others before myself?" J.J. could only humbly nod his head.

A day after the investigation, I was released back to the general population (by God's grace, twenty-nine days early, with no IDC punishment). The inmates were amazed at my courage.

While I was in the bathroom, an inmate named Hipolito (nicknamed Hippo because he was about 450 lbs.) came up to me and said, "I'm so sorry, man. I was the one who wrote those words about Smith on the wall. I can't believe you sacrificed yourself for me."

I hugged him and told him, "It's okay, brother. I love you, man. I knew that God was going to watch over me and protect me for a righteous act, although my objective was to show J.J. the love of Christ through my sacrifice for you."

That one act of love changed not only J.J., Hippo, Mr. Smith, and many inmates, but the rewards that I received for following God's purpose also can't be measured. What a world it would be if everyone put others before themselves.

Plea Deal

It was on 7/19/07, four days before I was scheduled to go to trial, when I received a call from a public defender. It was the call I had been anticipating ever since the visit from the one-toothed chaplain. This time, it was someone new and one of those moments over the course of a lifetime that you never forget.

She started the conversation by saying, "I have good news."

"What is that?" I responded.

"They have agreed to drop all the felonies to misdemeanors and are offering a year and a day in prison or 364 days in the county jail, which includes time served if you'll agree to complete the drug program and anger management, as well as two years of supervised probation."

That was a no-brainer. To go from possibly seven to ten years in prison to one year . . . are you kidding me? I needed the drug program anyway, and since I had already served six months, that meant I would only be incarcerated less than another five months with good behavior and gain time subtracted from my sentence.

I chose county jail over prison because I was comfortable there and knew prison could be much farther away depending on where they decided to send me, and there would be less chance of my sons visiting me.

Quite possibly the best part about the deal was the opportunity to see a bit of the outside world. While in the pods, the only part of the outside world that we were blessed to see was the sky visible only from Cracker Beach. Now while having to go to classes, I would have the chance to leave the pod to walk outside under escort to the program's building. That might not sound very exciting, but when you've been confined to the interior of the four walls of the pods for over seven months (except when traveling in the paddy wagon in the dark early in the morning to attend court), the blessing of seeing palm trees and grass and smelling the fragrance of tropical flowers—things that I once took entirely for granted—I would now be able to cherish every day for eight weeks. Just the thought of inhaling the aroma of the Florida air had me dreaming about soon returning home.

I excitedly told her, "Sign me up!"

When I got off the phone, I went around the pod, yelling, "I told you they were gonna drop the charges! I told y'all! There ain't nothing God can't do!" My brothers all had big smiles and were almost as excited as I was.

The Light through the Roof

"**Y**our sons and daughters will prophesy, your old men will dream dreams, your young men will see visions" (Acts 2:17).

Technically, being forty-six years old, I was middle-aged and, hence, a young man and an old man.

Approximately four to five months into my stay, I began having amazingly brilliant lifelike dreams. Sometimes I'd remember them in the morning, but often, I'd forget them. So I began praying to God that after having a dream, He'd wake me up so I could remember it, and He was faithful. So I kept a notepad next to my bunk, and after each dream (or vision), He'd wake me up, and I began writing them down (I would end up with four blue-line pads full of them). It was happening every night. The difference between a dream and a vision is that a vision is a dreamlike experience while being awake.

It was 8/4/07 in 6 Alpha at the Falkenburg Jail when I had what I believe in my heart to be a powerful vision. It was well after midnight while all the inmates slept when I saw it: a light, no, a beam of light. It shined down through the steel roof of our pod. It was so bright that I couldn't see the roof, only the light. "Whether in the body (a dream or vision), or out of the body (a spiritual actuality) I do not know, God knows" (2 Cor. 12:2). But that beam of light (see Acts 9:3) consumed my entire body.

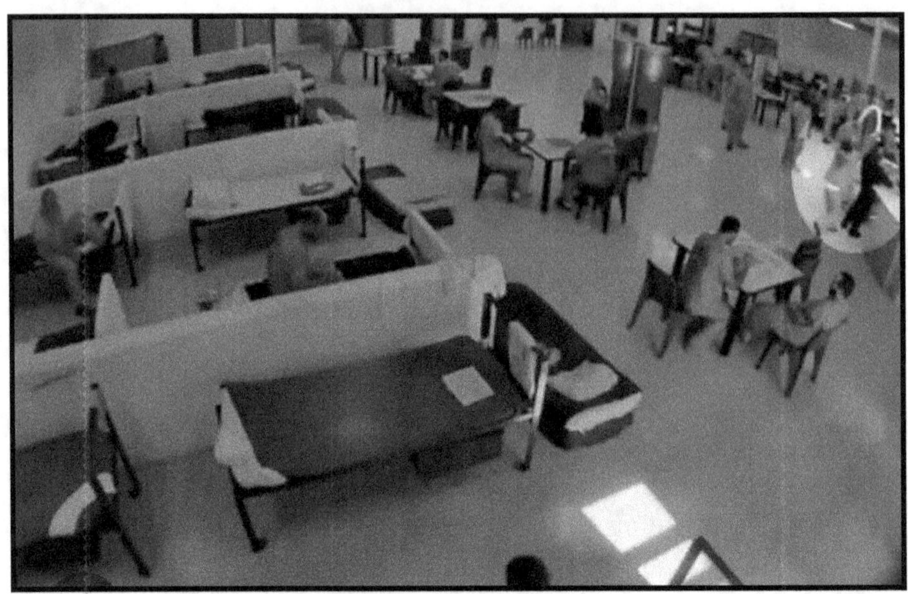

As the beam of light covered me and woke me, I looked down toward my feet as I felt my body being lifted off my bunk. Again, "whether in the body or out of the body I do not know, God knows" (2 Cor. 12:3–4). But as I lay there hovering about a foot or so above my bunk, I looked up into the beautiful light above me and said, "I'm ready, Lord" (to go home).

All He said was, "Not yet," and all I know is that I was still there in the morning to enjoy another scrumptious jailhouse breakfast.

I've only told two people about this (my mentor Pastor Bob Santilli and my son Adam), but now I'm telling you. I can still see and feel that light.

> Of such a one I will boast; yet of myself I will not boast . . . For though I might desire to boast, I will not be a fool; for I speak the truth. But I refrain, lest anyone should think of me above what he sees me to be or hears from me. And lest I should be exalted above measure . . . (2 Cor. 12:5–6).

I saw what I saw, and I heard what I heard.

Johnny Cochran

This is another of the life-changing lessons the Lord taught me in jail. It's about an eighteen-year-old young man named Cedric "Johnny" Cochran. He had spent most of his teen years in the system and was in the drug pod with me, sentenced to the drug program.

In jail, canteen was like gold. A couple of bags of root beer barrels (sixty cents each) would fetch two to three meals. On this particular canteen day, I had purchased two bags of barrels and put them in my bunk drawer, then proceeded out to Cracker Beach to read my Bible in the sun. When I came back a few hours later and looked in my drawer, my canteen was gone.

Cochran was a notorious "bubble gum bandit" (canteen thief) and was the only inmate hovering around the area that the barrels were stolen from. When he was seen sucking on barrels the next day, it was obvious he was the culprit.

Several inmates were pissed that the Preacherman had been ripped off, especially when they all knew I would have given the barrels to Johnny for nothing if he had only asked. The inmates wanted blood (literally)! They were going to turn Johnny in to the deputy until I talked them out of it. I explained to them why.

Anyone in the drug program, upon completion, was released from jail. Cochran had been in a while and had been telling everyone about going home to his mom and friends. I explained to the blood-thirsty inmates, "It's only two bags of root beer barrels. If I turn him in, he will have to start the program all over again, and they will add additional time to his sentence."

The inmates argued that if I didn't turn Cochran in, then that would give him the opportunity to rob other inmates, which was a pretty convincing argument. I sat down the infuriated inmates and explained what the Lord Jesus taught regarding situations like this. Jesus said, "From him who takes away your goods, do not ask them back" (Luke 6:30) and "turn the other cheek" (Luke 6:29). Jesus even took it a step further when He said, "From him who takes away your cloak (coat), do not withhold your tunic (shirt) either," meaning when someone takes something from you, not only forgive them, but also give them something else. Apostle Paul referred to this practice as "heaping hot coals of fire on his head" (Rom. 12:20). What does that mean? It means to do something that will shock that person.

The natural reaction a person who does not have a personal relationship with Christ would have when being stolen from is anger and revenge. Jesus taught us to love and forgive. Jesus calls us to react in a "supernatural" way. To heap hot coals on people is to hopefully get them to think to themselves, "Why was he nice to me after what I just did to him?" Remember, we are to glorify God (1 Cor. 10:31–33) by being Christian examples to others in an effort to draw them to God. The natural reaction is to treat "evil with evil."

First Peter 3:9 says, "not returning evil for evil," and to the contrary, "overcome evil with good" (Rom. 12:21). This display of love and forgiveness is very important. It is what separates a true follower of Christ from the rest of the world. It's important because many are turned away from the church and Christianity because of displays of hypocrisy. We must walk the walk if we are going to talk the talk. I told my brothers often to be very careful because others were watching us Christians, just waiting for us to slip up.

Back to the Cochran story. I wanted to teach Cochran and the other inmates a lesson they would never forget. Cochran had asked me if I knew who stole my candy, and I told Johnny, "Yes, I know who did it."

Johnny became edgy and asked, "Are you gonna turn him in?" When I said no, Johnny was shocked ("hot coals on his head") and asked why not. I informed him that my God is a God of love and forgiveness.

The next day, I gave Johnny a bag of chips for free and gave him a big smile to go with it. Again, hot coals. The inmates still could not believe I was doing this.

A few days after this incident, when the deputy was calling the list of names out for church service on Sunday, guess who had signed up? Yes, Cedric "Johnny" Cochran. He began attending regularly and, on one Sunday, accepted Christ as his Savior.

This story is a perfect example of what planting seeds and being a godly example is all about. You just never know when one is going to land on good ground, take root, and produce fruit.

$1.20 is a very small price to pay to save one's soul from eternal death. Also, remember that "whoever has been forgiven little loves little" (Luke 7:47), so it can also be said the more you forgive a person, the more that person will love you. Cedric and I became very good friends.

Officer Robinson

The last pod I stayed in prior to my release was referred to as the "drug pod." It's interesting that it was also 6 Bravo, the same as the first home I had in Orient Road but at Falkenburg. It housed all the inmates who were sentenced to the Substance Abuse Program, and upon completion, the majority were released back into the world with only a couple of guys awaiting transfer "up the road" to prison.

One of the deputies there was an Officer Robinson. He wasn't very nice and had a distinct dislike for anything about God and especially me. He liked to humiliate me over the loudspeaker when I was trying to hold Bible studies. He'd announce, "Break it up, Mr. Holier than Thou."

On one particularly evil day, he was on a mission. He went from bunk to bunk, taking away everybody's Bibles (I hid mine in my pants) and proceeded to throw them outside the pod onto the ground and proudly announced, "We're gonna have a Bible-burning tonight!"

However, even though I knew he was merely antagonizing us, I immediately filed a formal complaint against him with the Internal Disciplinary Committee. He was free to insult me all he wanted, but I wasn't about to let him insult my God. The next day, everyone received their Bibles back.

I was diabetic, and although I was off my meds, I was now suffering from low blood sugar, which was an absolute blessing because I was given a morning and evening snack (a bologna sandwich and a carton of milk). Did I mention I was the only inmate who received two snacks a day?

On the strangest of nights, my good friend Deputy Robinson summoned me to his desk. When I got there, he jumped in my face.

"What is this?" he asked as he pulled out a huge basket of food! It contained fried chicken, hamburgers, bologna sandwiches, several packs of cookies, and other assorted goodies. Then he showed me it was addressed to David "Preacherman" Gaskill. I was astonished! It was truly another miracle as any food must pass through multiple security checks, so there was no logical explanation for the goodie basket.

God had been showing up for me my entire stay in jail, but this was truly an amazing display of His power and favor. Mr. Robinson wasn't amused in the least. He said he was gonna "get to the bottom of this" and then took the basket away and refused to give it to me.

I must have had the most amazing smile on my face as I strolled back to my bunk. I remember several inmates chiding me and saying, "There's no way he's giving you that food, man." I sat on my bunk and praised God like never before. I told Him that if it was His will for me to get that basket, then amen, but if not, I would still praise Him for once again showing me that He was with me.

Although an inmate informed me that Robinson had put the basket into the fridge, he didn't give it to me that night.

The next morning, after our 5:00 a.m. breakfast, when we were all back on our bunks, possibly the most powerful display of the Holy Spirit occurred.

As I lay on my bunk, Robinson came walking across the pod carrying the basket that he himself took the trouble of heating up and personally served it to me in bed. Talk about room service! The inmates were all in shock, and so was I. I took a piece of chicken, a milk, and some cookies, then proceeded to share the food with the guys in my quad. God is so good.

The Completion of the
Drug Program

It was a couple of days before Thanksgiving 2007 and the completion of the substance abuse program, which meant nearly all of us in the pod, except for a couple of guys who would be going up the road to finish longer sentences, would be going home to enjoy Thanksgiving dinner. Obviously, we were all very excited and began packing up our belongings.

I called my sons to inform them that I'd call them as soon as I was released so they could pick me up.

The deputy began calling out the names one by one to line up at the door to be transported to get their property and head home. One by one, they were called . . . everyone but myself.

I was getting a strange feeling in my spirit, so I approached the deputy to see what was up. That's when I got the stunning news that somehow, with absolutely no explanation, my sentence had been extended until March. I was thoroughly confused and terribly disappointed. It had been nearly ten months since I was able to do the one thing that I enjoyed more than nearly anything else in this life: hug my precious sons. I called them to let them know I wasn't going to be released quite yet. I did my best to mask my pain.

I also remembered what the one-toothed chaplain had told me about how "God could change records in the computer." Well, I wasn't so sure it was God who wanted me to remain in paradise, but He certainly allowed it, so there must have been a good reason.

I called Jean to see what I could find out, and she said she'd file a motion to get me in court as soon as possible since my sentence was to have ended once I completed the program. What exactly did God have up His sleeve?

I stayed focused. I spent most of my free time in solitude, sitting out on Cracker Beach, suntanning, exercising, reading the Word, and meditating on the Lord. Cracker Beach was my sanctuary, my Holy of Holies, if you will. It was where I was closest to God and could commune with Him without the distractions that were continual in the dorm. It was where I spent nearly all my free time.

I continued spreading the gospel, having Bible studies and prayer circles, and loving on my brothers until the good Lord decided that my foundation in Christ was solid enough to go home.

Chaplaincy Training

Possibly one of the most amazing and fascinating aspects of my stay at Orient Road and Falkenburg Universities was my transformation from being "the worst addict" my substance abuse counselor, Mr. Dunn, said he had ever seen, a man who, he confessed he felt had no chance, to a person whom everyone, from the inmates, doctors, nurses, officers, and deputies saw something very special in.

I was a soldier for the Lord during my incarceration. I was not only having church services but Bible studies and prayer circles on a daily basis.

Possibly, they respected my steadfastness, but it must be completely attributed to the work of the Holy Spirit. He was moving everywhere throughout the jail.

When I first arrived, I never saw anyone reading a Bible or praying on their knees, but suddenly, it seemed like a wave had flowed over the entire jail, and there were guys reading the Word everywhere and praying on their knees in every pod I was blessed to stay in.

Inmates began confiding in me almost as early as a couple of days after the miracle of 2/7/07, but to think that several employees of the jail were coming to me, an inmate charged with six felonies, for spiritual guidance still is hard for me to comprehend.

I had a deputy call me into his office, and he broke down in front of me, confessing that his wife had breast cancer, and it wasn't looking good, and he pleaded for me to pray for them, which I promptly did with all my heart.

I had another deputy confess with tears in his eyes that he was addicted to steroids (apparently, several deputies were as well) and didn't know what to do and also requested prayer.

Anytime there was an inmate who was acting up, they would call in the nurses and psych doctors to talk to them, and they would, in turn, come to me and ask me if I could get them under control, which I always did, and rather easily by the grace of God.

During my year in jail, I can honestly say, except for the hindrance of a couple of evil deputies, I was treated like a king by everyone within those barbwire fences . . . there's no other way to describe it but God.

Time to Go Home

On 12/19/2007, I was awakened at 4:00 a.m. to grab a bite to eat and then get shackled up with a couple of other guys for the luxury limo ride downtown to court. I wasn't exactly sure what was going on, but sensed it was a special day.

When we got to the courthouse, we were ushered into a cold, dark, stinky holding cell containing ten to twelve other anxiety-filled of the world's despised to wait a few hours for our call.

While we sat there in complete silence, the Lord prompted me to offer my brothers a prayer. I stood up and quietly asked, "Do you guys wanna pray?" In unison, they all stood up and somberly formed a circle. We all held hands, bowed our heads, and I prayed for God to have mercy on all of us and to show us favor in the eyes of the judge.

I could feel their spirits lifted, and they all thanked me, and we hugged and soon were shackled together to head into court.

My case was called mid-morning. Jean stated my case eloquently, and the judge quickly made the decision to amend my sentence. I didn't understand all the legal mumbo jumbo, so I leaned over and asked Jean, "Am I going home?" She nodded, and I can't explain the emotions I felt. What a relief . . . what excitement.

I arrived back at Falkenburg late that afternoon, started packing, and waited for my name to be called. I waited and waited all day and into the evening. I kept approaching the deputy's desk to ask what was going on, but he had no clue. He said sometimes it took a while to process the paperwork, so I had no choice but to wait patiently and enjoy another jailhouse meal or two or three or four or five.

My name didn't get called until the morning of 12/21/07.

So many things were running through my head like pizza, soda, fries, and ice cream, things that had become almost an afterthought during my stay. Surprisingly, ESPN and sports, my former gods, were not even a thought. I didn't watch TV in jail except for an occasional Sunday church service if one was on. I didn't even watch the NBA Finals, which they blessed us with as a special treat, but of all the things I looked forward to experiencing on the outside, by far, the number one was hugging my sons. I couldn't wait to see them.

As I waited by the gate to be released, I had many mixed emotions. There were periods when I actually wasn't sure I wanted to leave. Would I be able to continue the same walk with Jesus that began in the wee hours of 2/7/07? I realized I would never get another opportunity in my lifetime to spend a year alone with Him in the presence of God with no distractions, worries, or fears, just me and Jesus. All my time there was spent with God, and His presence was so powerful. I wasn't sure if it was ever going to be the same again once I left my refuge called jail.

My year there was truly the greatest and most important year of my life.

I could see my brothers had mixed emotions as well. Some were smiling and filled with joy that I was finally being set free to go home to see my sons, yet others had their heads down and were terribly sad; possibly, like myself, they wondered if they were ever going to experience the same pure and powerful love of God that I also felt permeating throughout the jail during our stay there.

I had become a father figure to many whom had never felt a father's love, and maybe they worried they would never experience it again. I loved every single one of those men deeply, and the feeling was mutual.

The man who spent nearly three decades in bondage to addiction and his own evil flesh, the man who was filled with suicidal thoughts and even planned his death, the man who Christ gave freedom to his soul and broke the bondage once and for all was about to be set free into a dark world.

Then it happened. One by one, each inmate stood up and walked over to me almost in a line. They each took turns shaking my hand and hugging me. One at a time, they came. The day when "Red" Collier gave me a fist bump was long gone; they weren't embarrassed to say, "I love you."

At the end of the line was one of my closest friends, a guy named Desmond. He shook my hand strongly and hugged me and said, "Give that devil hell."

"You know that, brother," I responded.

The deputy turned to me and said, "They really respect you." "That's love, sir," I answered, smiling.

As the gate opened, he blurted, "I'll see you next time." I looked him squarely in the eyes and responded, "You won't see me again, sir."

He warned me, "I've seen a lot of mighty men fall. Eight out of ten come back in here."

I shook his hand and said, "Not this mighty man," and I turned and walked out, never to see Cracker Beach again.

Note: I became a chaplain at Tampa's University Community Hospital in March 2008, less than three months after my release, and I have been a voluntary speaker/chaplain at Falkenburg jail's substance abuse program since 2010; that's nothing but God.